Science
Stages 1
and Background

A Unit for teachers

Published for the Schools Council by
Macdonald Educational, London and Milwaukee

First published in Great Britain 1972 by
Macdonald Educational Ltd
Holywell House, Worship Street
London EC2A 2EN

Macdonald-Raintree Inc.
205 W. Highland Avenue
Milwaukee, Wisconsin 53203

Reprinted 1973 (with amendments), 1974, 1977, 1980

ISBN 0 356 04006 2

Library of Congress Catalog Card Number
77-83000

The chief author of this book is:

Don Radford

The other members of the Science 5/13 team are:

Len Ennever	Project Director
Albert James	Deputy Project Director
Wynne Harlen	Evaluator
Sheila Parker	
Roy Richards	
Mary Horn	

Made and printed by Waterlow (Dunstable) Limited

General preface

'Science 5/13' is a project sponsored jointly by the Schools Council, the Nuffield Foundation and the Scottish Education Department, and based at the University of Bristol School of Education. It aims at helping teachers to help children between the ages of five and thirteen years to learn science through first-hand experience using a variety of methods.

The Project produces books that comprise Units dealing with subject-areas in which children are likely to conduct investigations. Some of these Units include books of background information. The Units are linked by objectives that the Project team hopes children will attain through their work. The aims of the Project are explained in a general guide for teachers called *With objectives in mind,* which contains the Project's guide to Objectives for children learning science, reprinted at the back of each Unit.

Acknowledgements

The Project is deeply grateful to its many friends : to the local education authorities who have helped us work in their areas, to those of their staff who, acting as area representatives, have borne the heavy brunt of administering our trials, and to the teachers, heads and wardens who have been generous without stint in working with their children on our materials. The books we have written drew substance from the work they did for us, and it was through their critical appraisal that our materials reached their present form. For guidance, we had our sponsors, our Consultative Committee and, for support, in all our working, the University of Bristol. To all of them we acknowledge our many debts : their help has been invaluable.

Metrication

This has given us a great deal to think about. We have been given much good advice by well-informed friends, and we have consulted many reports by learned bodies. Following the advice and the reports wherever possible we have expressed quantities in metric units with Imperial units afterwards in square brackets if it seemed useful to state them so.

There are, however, some cases to which the recommendations are difficult to apply. For instance we have difficulty with units such as miles per hour (which has statutory force in this country) and with some Imperial units that are still in current use for common commodities and, as far as we know, liable to remain so for some time. In these cases we have tried to use our common sense, and, in order to make statements that are both accurate and helpful to teachers we have quoted Imperial measures followed by the approximate metric equivalent in square brackets if it seemed sensible to give them.

Where we have quoted statements made by children, or given illustrations that are children's work, we have left unaltered the units in which the children worked—in any case some of these units were arbitrary.

Contents

Games often remain unchanged for hundreds of years but toys come and go, evolve and develop and frequently reflect the spirit of the age

1 Toys educate: what the book is about

In myth and ritual the great instinctive forces of civilised life have their origin : law and order, commerce and profit, craft and art, poetry, wisdom and science. All are rooted in the primitive soil of play.'

Homo Ludens, J. Huizinga

Children's toys in Hammurabi's Babylon, showing knucklebones and tops

1.1 Toys: a human need

Nearly three and a half millennia ago the boy king Tutankhamen died and was buried in the Valley of Kings, accompanied by the treasures of his kingdom. His tomb was filled with the artifacts of his times and was perfectly preserved until re-discovered in 1922. This small sepulchre of a minor Egyptian king was untouched by the grave robbers and so it yielded secrets which astounded the world. Amongst the artifacts of life three and a half thousand years ago were toys of the children living at the time : toys like draughts, dolls and figures, even mechanical toys which moved their limbs when a cord was pulled. Evidently the trade of the toy maker was flourishing even then.

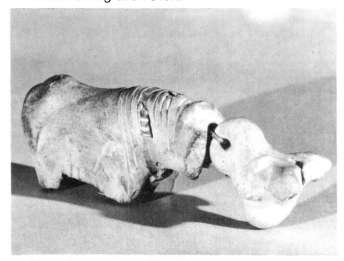

Harrapan clay toy, Indus valley c 2700 BC

Four thousand years ago the children of Hammurabi's Babylon played with clay rattles, tops and knucklebones. Even further back in time, in the valley of the Indus, some four and a half thousand years ago, children played with toys. Relics found include clay rattles, dolls, small animals and even an animal with a movable head worked by pulling a string. Once again, there is evidence to suggest that these were made by professional toy makers. When we dig into the spoil heaps of past civilisations

Egyptian wooden animal with movable jaw, Thebes c 1000 BC

we find the remains of toys. In some form or other, toys seem to be, and to have been, universal.

Children make their own toys out of anything going, and sometimes, in their own direct way, ignore the sophisticated 'super' toys, preferring their own creations. But, of whatever kind they are, toys seem to fill a niche in the child's world; they are the instruments of his play in which actuality and imagination are inextricably mixed.

Grown-ups play—they call it a hobby—and, of course, they need tools, instruments or equipment for their play, but they won't admit to calling these toys; indeed, playing with them they call work. We all seem to require some form of recreation or play; now that a working week of thirty hours is forecast as being a possibility in the next twenty years, leisure time pursuits for adults are just as important as playtime for children.

1.2 How the Unit is arranged

This Unit has no grand theme but is built up from a number of case histories, each one connected with a particular toy. Sometimes a toy, such as a doll, has been used in a number of schools; in that case the information has been combined and a general pattern produced.

In each section, sufficient background material is given so that teachers can see where suggested lines of development can lead, and immediate information is provided regarding the science which is involved. No attempt has been made to separate Stages 1, 2 & 3 work, but teachers are urged to select only work which is appropriate for their pupils. Child-based work is printed in rust brown

1.3 Some points raised by teachers

Teachers working with toys have said that children need to be helped along, at least to begin with, by asking them suitable questions. This is not surprising because if children, by themselves, could have developed scientific ideas by playing with toys there would be little point in bringing them to school. The real nub is what questions should be asked and, of course, the discussions which follow. There is no substitute for discussion with pupils in order to find out what they understand and to help them clarify their ideas : work cards will not do it.

Work of this nature, which requires a certain measure of guidance, probably needs to be carried out in small groups while the rest of the class is doing something else. For children who are familiar with group working this mode of activity will present few problems, but children who are not used to class activities may have to receive a good deal of help to get them started. However, once an investigation is under way, the teacher could return to the rest of the class for the time being.

It is often useful to introduce freer methods gradually, having several groups working freely while the rest of the class continue in their usual way, with a rota so that everyone has a chance to try group working. Difficulties which arise from group working are discussed in the Unit *Metals Stages 1 & 2* and are repeated below in 1.7.

1.4 How science comes from toys

Sometimes the toys themselves provide the material for the scientific work, for example, in measuring speeds of toy trains; on other occasions a toy such as a doll's house, simply gives the starting point and the work goes on from there. Another example of this development is the work on sound which started with a ventriloquist's doll.

It should not be thought that scientific investigation will automatically develop from toys and play. A bright child might have a flash of inspiration but generally it isn't until the teacher asks the 'right' question and provides the 'right' environment that the child stops, thinks and then begins to wonder. This places a heavy responsibility upon the teacher who has to know fruitful lines of development and how to guide pupils until they take up the quest. Fortunately the initial interest is already there, but no one is pretending that the task is a simple one.

Sometimes the act of play produces experiences which in themselves are scientific experiences although the child may not recognise them as such, but later these experiences may be drawn upon in a completely different context, for example, the winding of a clockwork car is an example of the storage of energy and may be referred to at a later date.

To summarise, toys may provide: i. starting points for investigations, ii. material to be investigated immediately, iii. experiences which may prove of value in the future.

1.5 Toys and construction

Another aspect of toys is that of construction. Here the child starting with simple common everyday materials builds something in which he is interested and in doing so he may have to solve practical problems of construction and design. Some highly original designs have been made by children in overcoming difficulties which adults may not see or, if they did, would solve in a completely different way. Construction work, for example making hulls of boats of different shapes, does provide, as one teacher said, 'An opportunity for discussion about the need to use tools properly.'

Sometimes the often despised and criticised plastic kits have their place: they may encourage a child to be patient, to read and follow a set of instructions and sometimes they produce an item which to him is aesthetically satisfying.

The highest level of toy and model making is the designing and construction from raw materials of something which interests the child. Most likely the design and construction will go hand in hand as often it does in adult life (watching builders put up a house is a lesson in approximating and making things fit), but it is the frequent problems and the solving of them which is both stimulating and satisfying to a child. Nothing succeeds like success and if children can solve their problems, maybe with a little unnoticed help, they are encouraged to go on. Difficulties are meant to be overcome, not shelved, and it would be sad to see work started with high hopes and then abandoned because of some difficulty which might easily be resolved with a little mature guidance.

1.6 Background material

An attempt has been made to include sufficient background material for the teacher but in some cases this information contains ideas and concepts which make it unsuitable for children unless it is suitably 'translated' for them. Also there has been no attempt to separate the background from the practical work so that a certain amount of discrimination is needed to avoid the presentation of what may be to children, something that is indigestible.

1.7 Teaching techniques

1.7.1 Discussion
Whatever method of teaching is used the teacher has a most powerful tool when interest wanes. Discussion between child and child, or between child and teacher is of the utmost importance, but it is necessary that any discussion should be skilfully managed so as to avoid any impression that it is a lesson in disguise or that the teacher is telling the children what to do. Discussion is the middle and both ends of our work and without it work, except with gifted children, is likely to fizzle out. Skilfully maintained discussion can initiate a host of ventures and help to sustain them through difficult periods by digging deeper and throwing up interesting ideas.

1.7.2 Records
Work of the kind we have discussed gives scope for records of many kinds. Children have expressed themselves through written accounts of what they have done, through poems they have written, models they have made and pictures they have painted. They have used charts and graphs to express the results of their investigations. Such work should be encouraged and because they have gained first-hand experience through working with toys, children find themselves in the position of having something to say or express. They can

Boat in gutter.

A method devised by children of recording the pattern of waves made by a boat being towed along a 6 in plastic gutter filled with water (see 6.3.1). The waves are represented by string stuck on to a strip of black paper.

do so with authority because they have had personal experiences—it happened to them.

Certainly the recording of observations needs to be encouraged but the type and format could be left largely to the pupils' choice aided in some measure by the teacher who knows what is appropriate for the children and for the material being recorded. There is no reason why a tape recorder can't be used if it is available : many children will make far more use of the spoken rather than the written word when they leave school. To marshal facts, and present arguments clearly are just as difficult to a speaker as to a writer. The main difference is that the speaker is relieved of the mechanical chore of writing: however, he might be well advised to marshal his facts in *NOTE* form before he starts to speak. Many children are inhibited from making records because they lack the manual dexterity and spelling skills needed of a writer.

1.7.3 Integration
Once more a plea is made to integrate science with other subjects—let it be a two-way process, so that science topics could be investigated and discussed during the course of other studies. If a science topic leads on to other studies, all well and good. A case in point is the use of a study of metals in helping to develop a child's vocabulary. At first glance this may not seem to be relevant to a science study but all subjects, science included, depend upon a working vocabulary and every opportunity should be taken to make sure that children have a working experience of words and phrases outside their own often limited everyday sphere.

1.7.4 Class management during the change from formal class teaching to informal working in groups
To some teachers who have been used to teaching in a formal situation, the ideas of group working present a number of difficulties. To go from formal teaching to group working cannot be done overnight. Not only is the classroom arrangement different but also the attitudes of the children are different. If children are used to a classroom in which they carry out directed work it would be hard for them to change over quickly to a situation in which they are largely responsible for their own activities. The change-over must be gradual, say one group at a time. If one group is successful perhaps its members could be used to head other groups and so the change is made progressively with some children in group work and some in more formal classwork. One decision the teacher has to make is 'How do I formulate the groups?' Should the basis be one of ability or of friendship? Allowing children to form friendship groups of about three or four members usually means that

they will themselves form groups in which the members do not widely differ one from another in their likes and dislikes and their abilities.

1.7.5 Work cards
The advisability of whether to use work cards or not must be left to individual teachers. Cards have the advantage that the teacher can attend to other children while the work card group is carrying on with their investigations and there is no reason why a work card cannot pose open-ended questions and not be just a 'cook-book'. If teachers guard against the obvious disadvantages and constantly revise the cards, weeding out those cards and sections which are unsuitable for various reasons, then they may well prove to be a useful teaching tool especially during the transition period of change from 'formal to free'.

One serious disadvantage of cards, is that they take a long time to prepare and they need to be slanted to meet the needs of the children using them. The time factor is a serious one but can be met if teachers of children working on a common theme meet together and thrash out basic ideas. (Cards could be slightly altered to meet local conditions.)

1.7.6 Discovery work
At no time has it been suggested that everything should be learned only by 'practical discovery'—all the various forms of teaching can play their part. Suggesting to a child that he finds out something in a book is just as valid as a visit to a cathedral or a piece of formal teaching. Each has its place, each is an effective tool when used in the right way at the right time. In this Unit not all the activities are practical discoveries; there are quite a number of 'looking', 'reading' and 'asking' things to do. In so doing, a child discovers something new to him; *he* has made the step forward; he himself has found out something. The important point is the motivation of the child not the actual method of finding out.

1.8 The Unit and objectives: what the numbers in the margins mean

The Unit contains suggestions for things children might do when exploring and investigating a particular subject area: these are easily recognisable.

It also contains objectives since one aim of the Project is to encourage teachers to work 'with objectives in mind'. These are less easy to recognise, and their function in the unit is not so apparent as the children's activities. Here we set the scene for objectives but we strongly recommend that teachers read the book *With objectives in mind* for fuller understanding.

Broadly speaking, objectives are statements about what children might achieve from their work. They occur throughout the Unit, explicitly stated or implicitly there.

1.8.1 Recognising objectives in the Unit
The *Statement of objectives for children learning science* will help. You will find this at the back of the book. It is reprinted from *With objectives in mind* and all objectives in the Unit are taken from it.

There are two things to notice about the statement:

i. The objectives have a particular arrangement based on their relationship to the Broad Aims * of the Project and to the stages of children's development which we have called Stages 1, 2 and 3.

ii. The objectives are numbered to indicate this relationship. The system of numbering is simple:

* *You will find a diagram of the Broad Aims and an explanation of the Stages accompanying the statement on pages* 83-89.

the *first* digit	indicates whether an objective is at Stage 1, 2 or 3.
the *second* digit	indicates the Broad Aim under which the objective is located.
the *third* digit	identifies the individual statement.

For example: the objective *ability to construct models as a means of recording observations* is numbered *2.74*. The number *2.74* has the following meaning:

2
This shows the stage in children's development to which the objective chiefly applies—in this this case Stage 2

.7
This shows the broad aim to which the objective is expected to contribute   in this case *.70 Communicating*

4
This shows the position (arbitrary) in the list of Stage 2 objectives that contribute to *Communicating*

The numbers are useful labels, allowing easy reference to a particular objective without quoting it in full. They do not imply any order of priority among objectives.

1.8.2 In some Units the numbers in the margins of the text will help
You will notice numbers in the margin of this text. These are the numbers of objectives from the main statement that are relevant if children embark on the suggested work. They are included to help teachers think about objectives implicit in particular situations.

1.8.3 The index to objectives will help

You will find this at the back of the book. It relates to objectives occurring in the Unit listed against the pages on which they occur. The lists are preceded by an explanatory introduction to the index which indicates how it can be used within the Unit and also in conjunction with the Guide to objectives for children learning science extracted from *With objectives in mind* and reprinted on page 82 of this Unit.

These three sources of information will help you to work 'with objectives in mind'.

Children's games, reproduction of a painting by Pieter Brueghel the Elder . How many games can you recognise?

Using our ears

Looking at ourselves—Our Ears

Infant work arising from playing with toy cars

Lino prints based on cog-wheels.

2 Looking at toys: where is the science? Background information for teachers

What science is there in toys? Can we say that such and such a toy may be helpful in developing a particular idea? The following sections illustrate the science which lies hidden in toys; many of the ideas require adapting before they are introduced to children. They are given to show you what lies behind a toy, and in some cases the principles which govern its working. The toys which are examined in this Unit are:

spinning toys,

toys which make a noise, or sounds,

toys which use pumps,

'gravity' toys,

inertia toys,

toys which move,

construction toys,

models and structures.

2.1 Spinning toys

The figure below shows at *a* a top, common in the period between the two World Wars. It was known to the children of London as a 'Flying Angel' or a 'Flying Dutchman' because with a strong whip it could be made to fly a considerable distance.

What factors go to make a good top?

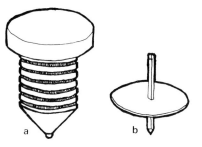 

Tops may be spun with a whip (a) or between finger and thumb (b) and (c)

Probably we have made a spinner, a form of dice for some kind of game. These are easily made from a piece of cardboard and a match-stick, tooth-pick, cocktail stick or lollipop stick, but how about trying to make a 'better' spinner. What could be used for the disc? Does the size or weight matter? How about using Plasticine to load the cardboard disc; does it matter where the Plasticine is put? Can a better material be used in place of the match-stick? Does the end have to be sharp or blunt? Why? Does the surface on which it is spun have any effect?

At the heart of the matter two scientific principles are involved; one deals with friction and the other with inertia. A body tends to stay at rest or keep moving unless something interferes with it. (This is one of Newton's Laws.) Friction tends to slow down a spinning disc, inertia tends to keep it spinning. How can we increase the inertia and decrease the friction? That is the real problem.

The importance of inertia is seen again in fly-wheels, yo-yos, diabolos, gyroscopes, and those toy cars which keep going when pushed because a heavy fly-wheel inside them has been made to spin very fast by the initial push.

2.2 Toys using springs

The toy car mentioned in 2.1 stored energy (let us call it *go*) in its fly-wheel. A spring is a very convenient method of storing or absorbing *go* which can then be released at a suitable time and in a suitable manner.

If we look at toys with springs we find quite a range : there are those which pop up like a Jack-in-the-Box ; those which wind up ; those which shoot, like an air gun, a crossbow or a long-bow. Then there are those which make use of the spring of elastic such as catapults and rubber motors in model aircraft. All these toys can present problems for children to find out about, and mechanisms and devices for them to explore. How is the 'run down' of a spring in a wind-up toy regulated ? What part does air play in an *air* gun ? How many different *kinds* of springs are used in toys ? Are they all used for the same purpose ? Are they all made in the same way ? What are they made of ?

Springs are used in everyday life in many different ways ; eg for beds and for car suspension. (What about the cars which do not have conventional suspension springs but use air or water ?)

2.2.1 The cotton reel tank, an example of storing energy

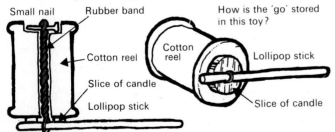

Small nail   Rubber band

How is the 'go' stored in this toy ?

Cotton reel

Cotton reel   Lollipop stick

Cotton reel

Slice of candle

Lollipop stick   Slice of candle

The tank engine is a twisted rubber band

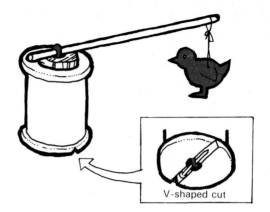

If the cotton reel is stood upright it can act as a merry-go-round

2.2.2 The modern tank, using a squeezy bottle

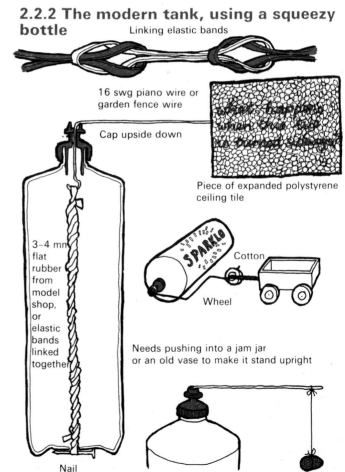

Linking elastic bands

16 swg piano wire or garden fence wire

Cap upside down

Piece of expanded polystyrene ceiling tile

SPARKLO   Cotton

Wheel

3–4 mm flat rubber from model shop, or elastic bands linked together

Needs pushing into a jam jar or an old vase to make it stand upright

Nail

What can be done with a toy like this?

i. Using it as a run-about toy.

a. How fast will it go?
b. How far will it go with 20 winds? with
40 winds? with 60 winds? etc.
c. What is the steepest slope it will climb?
Can we prevent 'wheel-spin'? How do you
measure slopes?
d. Will the toy pull things (eg trucks) along?
(It will need modifying otherwise it will go in
circles—why?)
e. What happens if the 'toy' is put on a very
smooth slope?

ii. Using it as a merry-go-round.

a. How many times will it go round in a minute
if the expanded polystyrene tile is — ▭ ?
If the expanded polystyrene tile is flat — ▭ ?
Are we being fair? Should we make sure that
the merry-go-round is wound up to the same
extent each time?
b. What happens if a thread and a lump of
Plasticine is tied on the end of the wire?

What is the science in this toy?

First of all it can be used to introduce or
reinforce ideas on distance, time and speed.

Then there is the storage of go or energy—what
makes the toy go?

Other scientific ideas which might be
investigated:
slopes, how they are measured,
air resistance,
something which is commonly called centrifugal
force,
friction—if the floor is very smooth, the toy spins
as if it had wheel-spin.

Through playing (or working) with toys like
these, children gather experience which they
may add to later experiences and from them
distil scientific principles. It is not intended that

these early experiences should provide the only
support for the scientific ideas mentioned, they are
merely introductory, but it may help the child
later if these ideas are referred to by name now.

2.3 Toys which make noises, sounds or music

Children seem to delight in making noises; at
first almost any noise will do, then come

when my daddy chops wood
I can see him and then I can hear
him chopping wood

An observation made by a child in an Infant school during some
work on sound which arose out of 'playing' with simple musical
toys and instruments

attempts at rhythm and musical notes.
Fortunately there are a number of simple
musical instruments which can be made by
children using everyday materials.

Sounds are usually caused by something
vibrating which in turn causes the air to vibrate.
However, sound will travel through substances
other than air, and children have rung bells
under water and sent messages along pipes.
They have also tried to measure the velocity of
sound by measuring how long it took the sound,
made by banging two blocks of wood together,
to cross a playing field.

Vanessa Brazier   Wednesday 20th November

How fast sound travels

Yesterday afternoon Marcelle Susan Janet and I went to the recreation ground to see how fast sound travels. Janet and Susan stood at one end with the horn and the books and Marcelle and I stood at the other end with the stop watch and the trundle wheel. As soon as Susan blew the horn she would put her hand up and as soon as I saw it I would start the stop watch and as soon as I heared the sound I would stop the stop watch and see how long it took the sound to get to me. Then Marcelle would measure the distance between Susan and Janet and Marcelle and I. We changed ends because the wind might be going against the sound or the same way as the sound. We had lots of results and this was our average results.

Resutls

Distance = 600 ft
Time lapse between signal and sound = $\frac{1}{5}$ sec.
Therefore in $\frac{1}{5}$ of a sec sound travels 600 ft
In $\frac{1}{5}$ sec sound travels $\frac{600ft}{6} = 100ft$

Therefore in one whole sec sound travels   100 × 10 = 1000ft

An attempt to measure the speed of sound by children of nine to ten

Ideas which children may be able to develop might be:

i. What makes the sound?

ii. Rhythms.

iii. Musical notes (see the Unit *Metals Stages 1 & 2*, 4.3 vi).

iv. Vibration of things. Vibration of air (see 2.3.4). In a stringed instrument, the pitch of the note depends on the length and the tightness of the string.

2.3.1 Tapping
Large nails or pieces of brass, copper or iron tubing can be cut to different lengths with a hacksaw and arranged to give the notes of the octave when struck.

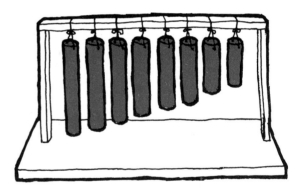

Tubular bells (see *Metals Stages 1 & 2* (4.3) vi.,)

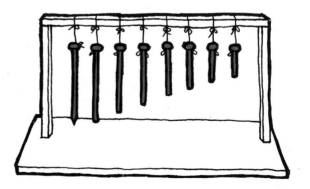

A xylophone is made of wooden bars of varying lengths laid across supports as shown in the figure below. Another possibility is to drive a series of large nails varying depths into a block of wood, as in the figure below. Is it better to lay the block flat, or to stand it on its edge? In carrying out an investigation like this when some thing or some action needs duplicating or repeating a number of times, it might be best to encourage different children or groups to do the repeats and then to compare their findings.

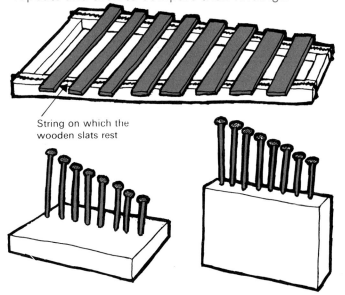

String on which the wooden slats rest

Six inch nails driven varying distances into a block of wood can also make an octave

---

* Instead of string, a good material is a sticky-back strip of plastic foam commonly used as a draught preventer.

Jam jars or milk bottles containing different amounts of water give different notes when struck.

Which gives the highest note? Which gives the lowest note? Is it the glass or the water which gives the note? Start with an empty jar.

2.3.2 Banging: let us make a drum
How many ways can children devise to make a drum? The hollow part can be a jar, an old saucepan, a wooden box, a tin; all shapes and sizes can be tried and different sounds produced. But it is the covering material for the open end which may give the most trouble. On a real drum it is usually parchment, which is made from skin, stretched tight, and it is this tightness which is important.

Materials which have been used and might be tried are: thin cotton or nylon cloth, thick wallpaper, plastic film such as thick polythene wrapping material, rubber sheeting. The cotton, nylon and wallpaper must be damped and stretched tight, tied in place with string and allowed to dry, then varnished with aircraft dope.

If small seeds (radish, mustard) are sprinkled on the drum (cf. *Early experiences*) and the drum then tapped the vibration of the skin can be seen.

2.3.3 Rattling
The maraca used in jazz, swing or Latin music bands was a rattle made from a dried gourd and containing seeds, beads or shot. The gourd

A maraca can be made from two yogurt cartons taped together with a few beans inside

can be replaced by a squeezy bottle or two yoghurt cartons taped together and a variety of rattling material can be tried (big beans, little beans, dried peas, sand, lentils).

2.3.4 Blowing
Basically there are two methods of producing a note by blowing; one is to make air vibrate (eg by blowing across the top of a tube or bottle); the second is to make something else vibrate. An example of this is the reed in some wind instruments which can be copied using a drinking straw. Various lengths of straws give different notes, but can you make different notes without altering the length of the straw?

Obtain a number of medicine bottles all of the same size. Pour different amounts of water in each bottle and blow across the tops of them; which bottle produces the highest note? Which produces the lowest note?

Compare the amounts of water in each bottle. Does the one with the least amount of water give the highest or lowest note?

Compare the results of this investigation with that of jam jars and water (2.3.2)—how can the results be explained? (In the case of the jam jars it is the glass above the water level which vibrates and the larger the amount of glass the lower the note. With the medicine bottles it is the air which vibrates and the more air there is, the lower the note.)

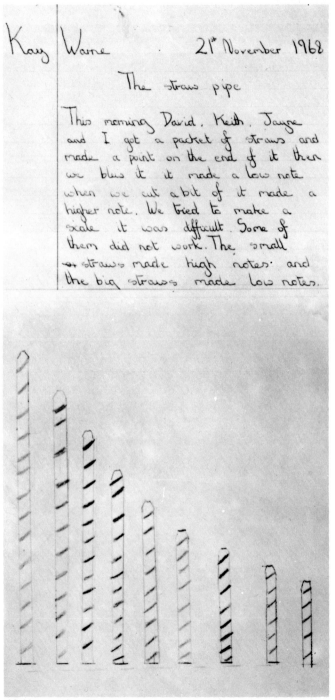

A simple reed instrument made from a drinking straw

2.3.5 Plucking
A banjo or guitar could be used to discover the change in note when the length of string and tension of string are varied. A number of home-made stringed instruments can be

Making music with a straw

constructed. Bowing a stringed instrument is only another way of inducing the strings to vibrate.

The frequency of a note given by a string is increased as the length of the string is decreased.

The frequency increases as the tension increases.

For the connection between a note and its frequency see *Metals Stages 1 & 2,* 4.3 vi.

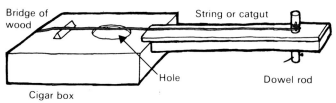

Home-made plucking instrument

2.3.6 Pop gun and cap pistol

The mechanism of the pop gun involves the compression of air and its sudden release causing an explosion. Could a silencer be made for a pop gun ? It would have to work in a manner similar to a car's silencer. (What does the silencer of a car do ? What is it like inside ? How does it work ?)

Why does a paper bag full of air bang when it is struck ? What makes the noise in a cap pistol ? This is really a small explosion produced by a chemical reaction. What is an explosion ? The noise of an explosion is made when air is moved very violently. A whip cracks when the movement of the tip of the lash exceeds the speed of sound—there is a miniature sonic boom.

2.3.7 A humming top

A humming top is a good toy to investigate. What makes it spin ? Why does it hum ? Can the humming be controlled ? How long will the top continue to spin ?—see 2.1.

2.3.8 A bull roarer

Children may have heard the wind whistling through the telephone wires. This can be imitated by a primitive aboriginal instrument called a *bull roarer.*

If this is swung around the head faster and faster a loud humming is produced.

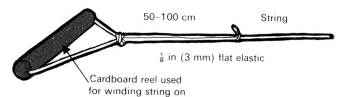

A bull roarer

2.3.9 Whistle

Some whistles have a pea in them. Do they work if the pea is removed ?

2.4 Toys and pumps

Most of us have used a bicycle pump at some time or other but there are a number of toys which make use of pumps.

2.4.1 Water pistol

Water pistols are of two types, the one-shot variety, and the repeater which sucks water from a holder and gives a number of squirts.

2.4.2 Pop gun or air gun

In a pop gun or air gun a spring, when released, forces a plunger to compress air in a barrel and this blows out some projectile. A simple form of this is the potato gun.

This consists of a length of tube about 20 cm long and a piece of stick which just fits inside the tube. One end of the tube is stuck in a potato. The piece of potato left in the tube is pushed further into the tube with the stick for 2—3 cm. The other end of the tube is then stuck into the potato and a piece left in the end of the tube. Now, if the stick is given a sharp and sudden push a potato plug will be fired from the other end of the gun. This used to be a favourite toy with which small boys used to annoy their sisters.

Potato plugs

Stick

Tube (copper, brass, aluminium)

The potato gun worked by compressed air

2.4.3 Where is the science?

Think about all the science to be found in simple toys. When water is sucked up by a pump what is it which causes the water to rise? It is the pressure of the air which forces the water up. From the simple pump in a water pistol we could look at pumps in everyday life—where are they and how do they work?

Here is a list of pumps:
bicycle pump
the heart (look at a sheep's heart, cut it open)
petrol and oil pumps in a car
vacuum cleaner
hair dryer
central heating water pump
hot air heater (car and some home electric heaters)
ventilation fans
pump used for blowing up a balloon

In nearly every case there is a device which allows the liquid or gas to go in one direction only—this is a valve (eg a bicycle tyre valve). What valves are used every day? Sometimes a gas or liquid is cleaned—how is this done? (Oil and air filters in a car; the bag in a vacuum cleaner.)

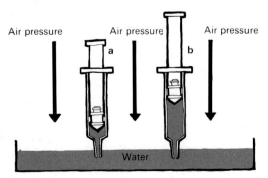

Air pressure   Air pressure   Air pressure

a   b

Water

Air pressure causes the rise of the water in the tube (provided that the piston gives an air-tight fit)

Why is the pop gun so called? Why does it go pop? Note the use of a spring to store energy in the air of the pop gun. Note also that air occupies space and is compressible whereas water does not seem to be compressible.

2.5 Toys and gravity

How many toys make use of the force of gravity (other than to just remain on the earth!)? Children unknowingly use the pull of gravity when they coast down hills on their bicycles or toboggans. They use it on the playground slides, bouncing balls, flying a paper dart, running model cars down slopes, or racing with their soap-box go-carts. In all these uses, gravity supplies the force which makes the thing go, or if you like, gives it 'go' or energy.

Sometimes the force of gravity is used to balance things as, for example, the pop-up clowns.

Try and knock over the pop-up man. How could you make it so that it returns if it is slightly pushed over, but remains over if it is knocked flat?

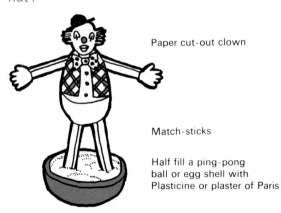

Paper cut-out clown

Match-sticks

Half fill a ping-pong ball or egg shell with Plasticine or plaster of Paris

A pop-up man

The keel of a yacht serves two purposes, to prevent the boat being blown sideways and to act as a balancing weight preventing the boat being blown over. So gravity comes in again.

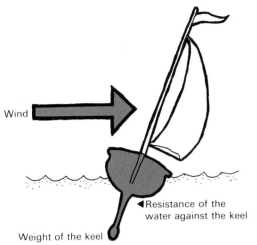

Wind

◄ Resistance of the
water against the keel

Weight of the keel

The keel of a boat gives resistance to sideways movement and its downward weight helps to balance the sideways force of the wind on the sails

A switchback can be made from a length of corrugated parcel paper draped over books. If a toy car is released at *A* will it reach *B* ? Does the *steepness* of the rise or ascent have any effect on how *high* the toy will go ? Can *B* be higher than *A* ?

A ball-bearing switchback (as in the figure below), made from curtain rail and a ball-bearing, illustrates the force of gravity and inertia. It can also be used to discuss the change of potential energy into kinetic energy (change from energy of position to energy of movement) and *vice versa*. What energy does the ball have at *A, B, C* and *D* ? (*A* = energy of position, *B* = energy of movement, *C* = energy of movement + energy of position, *D* = energy of movement.) Work on energy could most likely be tackled only by children who have made progress towards Stage 3. For the majority it is probably sufficient to have an experience of energy which they can make use of later. What slows the ball after passing *D* ? (Friction mainly between the rail and the ball-bearing.)

Gravity and the storage of *go* (energy) are demonstrated by the come-back-tin, which if you gently roll the tin away from you on the floor it returns under its own power.

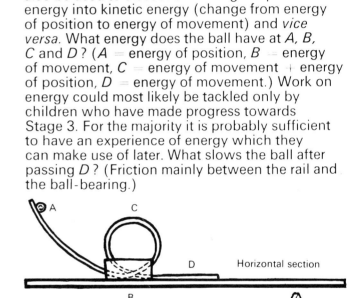

Horizontal section

The twisting elastic stores energy for the tin's return

The ball-bearing switchback

The principle of the switchback

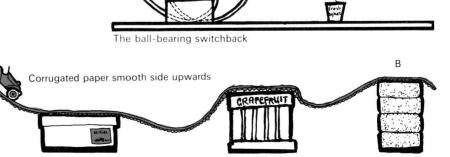

Corrugated paper smooth side upwards

A toy like Rockets, or Hot Wheels provides a track on which to run special low-friction model racing cars. It can be used to build up switchbacks similar to the ones shown on page 17 or a closed circuit can be used.

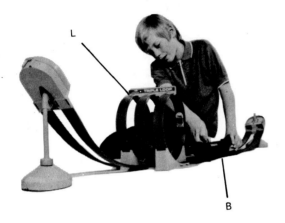

Photographs of a   Rockets   layout

B   booster, supplier of go
Bc   banked curves
H   hump-backed bridge
L   loop the loop

A toy like this can be used to provide experiences energy, friction and centrifugal force.

2.6 Toys involving inertia

Inertia is a property bodies have of either remaining at rest, or, if they are moving, of continuing to keep moving in a *straight line*, or, if they are spinning, of continuing to spin.

Children begin to appreciate inertia when they free-wheel their bikes, on a level stretch of road; when they try to turn a corner (why do so many accidents occur on corners?); when they roll a ball (why does it continue to move?); when they have a swing, or play with tops, fly-wheel toys or gyroscopes. Although inertia comes into so many toys, children are unlikely to appreciate it until their attention is focused upon it. Like metals and wood and the common materials around them, they do not *see* inertia until in some way they are made aware of it. This is where the teacher comes in with his discussions.

2.7 Toys which move from place to place

If we want to get from *A* to *B* in a vehicle, four problems confront us:

i. what method of transport shall we use?

ii. what is our source of energy to drive the vehicle?

iii. how do we use the energy?

iv. how shall we steer our vehicle?

Moving toys follow the same pattern.

The summary below is intended for teachers.

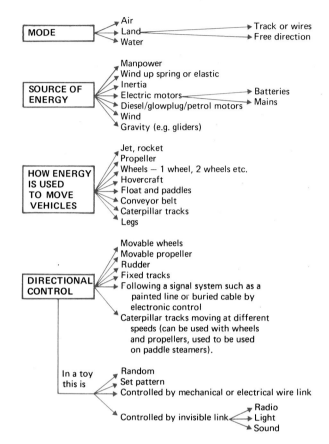

The whole aspect of transport in society can be illustrated and demonstrated in the classroom by toys ; so can the use of energy ; mechanical systems ; engines and a host of scientific ideas.

2.8 Construction toys

These are of two types : those which can be built up to form some toy and then can be taken to pieces to build something else ; those which when put together form a permanent structure. Meccano and Lego are examples of the first type, and plastic model kits are examples of the second type.

In any construction, the maker needs to know a number of things.

i. what is its purpose.

ii. what he is making will look like when finished.

iii. what tools and materials are needed.

iv. an idea of the stages in the building, and the order of the stages.

These are the things he needs to know *before* he starts. If he is skilled he will probably make sketches and work out dimensions for himself if they are not given. If instructions are given then he should be encouraged to read them through and through and to make sure that he understands plans, diagrams and written instructions. Impatience to get on with the job is understandable but it needs careful curbing. There is no room for a butterfly attitude in model construction ; one important firm asks its prospective apprentices if they are model makers and what they make so as to form some opinion of them.

Sometimes a model maker starts with raw material and has to design and fabricate his model entirely from scratch. Often problems arise during the building which have to be solved before continuing. It is the solving of these problems which makes model making such a satisfying occupation.

2.9 Models and structures

In a number of models, eg flying model aircraft, attention has to be paid to the strength of the structure in relation to its weight. This is quite a worthy field of study and reference should be made to the Unit *Structures and forces Stages 1 & 2.*

3 Some general objectives for toys

Many of the objectives which can collectively be applied to toys are those of a very general nature and are those which teachers may have in mind when dealing with any other topic. 'Willingness to ask questions or participate in group work' is a product of teaching not necessarily confined to the permissive classroom but is more likely to be evolved as a result of this way of teaching than in a formal atmosphere.

Although objectives are considered to be useful adjuncts for teachers, it is not suggested that they should mould the course of a child's work. It may be that in the course of a piece of work, the teacher may consider that a particular objective could be attained but the child, by following his own course irrespective of hints and environment, ends by achieving a totally different objective. The objectives which may exist in a teacher's mind are only possible goals, and not ones to be attained at all costs : the child at this stage is the real arbiter of the objectives which he can reach.

Besides the general objectives given here, more specialised objectives can be postulated for most of the toys dealt with in this book. *However, it should be emphasised that all these objectives are only put forward as suggestions, and that teachers are encouraged to think out and set up their own.* In this way teachers may be able to plan ahead and to structure the environment so that the laws of cause and effect can be put to good use instead of waiting for an advantageous situation to arise as the result of a random effect.

In the following paragraphs the numbers in colour refer to the objectives listed in the Guide to objectives (pages 83-89).

3.1 Some possible objectives for Stage 1

Willingness to ask questions.   1.01

Enjoyment in using all the senses for exploring and discriminating.   1.04

Willingness to collect material for observation or investigation.   1.05

Desire to find out things for oneself.   1.06

This means that we need to encourage children to be curious, to question what will happen and why, to be aware of things in their environment and as far as possible to be spontaneous in their activities.

Willing participation in group work   1.07

Toys provide many opportunities for group working in which tasks are shared and experiences communicated with other members of the class.

Appreciation of the need to learn the meanings of new words and to use them correctly.   1.09

Ability to use new words appropriately.   1.71

The topics related to toys naturally provide chances to introduce new words, not only of a technical nature but also of description and comparison.

Willing compliance with safety regulations in handling tools and equipment.   1.08

Some of the work with toys involves the use of tools for construction—it needs a measure of instruction, but whether this should be in the form of class demonstration or on a group basis is left to the discretion of the teacher. Certainly elementary rules, such as cutting away from you and not putting fingers in front of cutting instruments, need to be emphasised. This involves a certain requirement of discipline, and the children to realise that such 'rules' which are made are essential to themselves and their neighbours.

Awareness that there are various ways of testing out ideas and making observations.   1.11

Ability to use representational symbols for recording information on charts or block graphs   1.74

Ability to tabulate information and use tables.   1.75

Ability to record impressions by making models, painting or drawing.   1.77

These objectives all refer to the recording of work carried out. This recording can be in many forms and need not necessarily be in a written account. Children need encouraging to make permanent records because often they cannot see the value of such an exercise. If, on the other hand, they could be led to appreciate that their records may help their fellows, the task might become more acceptable. Furthermore, there is a large variety in the means of recording results of observations from a painting of a ship, to a graph or a model of a set of gear wheels.

Recognition of common shapes—square, circle, triangle   1.23

Quite a number of manufactured articles are built up of common shapes and it might be worthwhile identifying them. This might form the

basis of an art discussion.

Recognition of the action of force.   1.28

Appreciation that the ability to move or cause movement, requires energy.   1.58

Awareness of sources of heat, light and electricity.   1.56

Familiarity with sources of sound.   1.55

Usually the toys which go are the ones which arouse the most spontaneous interest. These are the toys which make use of energy. Energy is such an important concept and is the basis of much science. Here we have an opportunity to introduce —in a painless manner—all the common forms of energy change : eg chemical energy to sound (cap pistol) ; mechanical energy to sound (drums etc) ; electric energy to mechanical energy (train set) ; stored mechanical energy (spring) ; potential energy to kinetic energy (bouncing ball) ; kinetic energy to heat (friction) ; chemical energy to heat (flame) ; electrical energy to sound (radio set). Perhaps the changes are more rightly studied at a later stage, but a knowledge that a change takes place might be appropriate at an early stage, and such an awareness could come quite easily and naturally.

Awareness that more than one variable may be involved in a particular change.   1.44

This is well illustrated when trying to sort out why something will not work—very often everything is tried at once with resulting chaos. It takes some time and many examples for children to realise that a change in a situation is often complex and that a number of factors may be involved, either singly or in combination.

For example if a torch will not work it may be because of : a burnt out bulb, a run down battery, a broken switch, dirty contacts on battery, bulb or switch, or (in a two-battery torch), batteries put in back to front. The task is to find which are the relevant factors.

Appreciation of the need for measurement.　　1.43

This can easily be introduced when two things are compared: is John's engine faster than Robin's? or how much cloth does Mary require to make a dress for her doll?

Awareness of the meaning of speed and of its relation to distance covered.　　1.36

This is likely to be developed when considering speeds of trucks down an incline or trains or cars around a track.

3.2 Some possible objectives for Stage 2

Willingness to co-operate with others in science activities.　　2.01

This is an extension of the attitudes mentioned in Stage 1 in that the pupil is beginning to realise that two heads are better than one.

Enjoyment in examining ambiguity in use of words.　　2.04

As the pupil's vocabulary is increased he possesses a greater fluency and is able to express himself more ably; in so doing he will come across occasions when a sentence could be read to give more than one interpretation, or when his own explanations are ambiguous. It is good training to be pressed to say exactly what you mean.

Appreciation of measurement as division into parts and repeated comparison with a unit.　　2.31

Recognition of the role of chance in making measurements and experiments.　　2.94

By Stage 2, pupils are beginning to recognise the importance of measurements in their work and in many ways they genuinely like to measure things. The role of chance is not so easy to put over, but it does arise when considering the bouncing of ball-bearings on a block of metal.

Here the important point is that their results are not wrong because they do not always give the same answer.

Interest in choosing suitable means of expressing results or observations.　　2.05

Ability to use non-representational symbols in plans and charts, etc.　　2.71

Ability to use histograms and other simple graphical forms for communicating data.　　2.73

Ability to construct models as a means of recording observations.　　2.74

Once again this is only an extension of Stage 1 work and as the child develops so does his ability to communicate and to use more advanced forms of communication. This will show in his recording if it is encouraged.

Familiarity with a wide range of forces and ways in which they can be changed.　　2.52

Knowledge of sources and simple properties of common forms of energy.　　2.53

Appreciation of weight as a downward force.　　2.34

This is a natural progression from the start made in Stage 1, and will not only explore sources of the energy used in a toy, but also how that energy is put to use through gears and levers. At first there is almost an intuitive appreciation of energy, but little idea of how it is used. Now children can begin to trace the pathways from the source to the operation, eg in a clockwork toy, from the spring, through gears, to the wheels and to motion. An appreciation of the use of gears, as for example on a push bike, could be developed and perhaps even understood to a greater depth by the construction of a crane using gears.

Appreciation of the need to control variables and use controls in investigations.　　2.43

Ability to investigate variables and to discover effective ones.　　2.42

Ability to frame questions likely to be answered through investigations.   2.41

Having recognised the existence of variables in Stage 1, now comes the task of being able to sort them out. This means the beginnings of tackling a job in a systematic manner, so as to eliminate the unessential and to pin-point the effective. Having done so, then comes the job of asking the right questions; questions which help to lead to a solution of a problem. This type of work often arises with toys. If something is being made, several assessments are needed : what size ? what materials ? how can it be made ? what tools ? and so on. Or perhaps a toy breaks; why doesn't it work ? How can it be mended ?

Awareness of the changes in the physical environment brought about by man's activity. 2.85

Interest in the way discoveries were made in the past.   2.13

Awareness of some discoveries and inventions by famous scientists.   2.55

This is the spin off of toys : the relationship of the child's world of imagination to the real world, from the toy railway to the works of Brunel, from the jet car to the moon shot, and the works of Newton, from the building bricks to the shoe box skyscrapers of our cities, from the toy glider to the impact of Concorde. Perhaps some of these progressions are sophisticated, but year by year schoolchildren are becoming more and more sophisticated, more and more ready to accept the world as it is and less inclined to question and query our deeds and values. Is it not valid to begin to relate toys with the real world so that later moral, ethical and aesthetic judgements can be made ?

Skill in devising and constructing simple apparatus.   2.58

4 Dolls

4.1 Introduction and background

It seems that the earliest toys were dolls, although many may have been connected with religious rites and not used by children at all. Made of wood or clay and representing animals as well as humans, dolls have been known and played with for several thousands of years. Unfortunately few of these early toys have survived, but from medieval times we do have written records. Songs collected by German scholars contain references to dolls, hobby horses, marbles, hoops, tops and knucklebones. Pieter Brueghel the Elder painted *Children's Games* in 1539 and depicts some eighty games, many of which are familiar even to this day.

The German city of Nuremberg, famous for its craft guilds and as an important trading centre, built up its reputation on the production of wooden articles. From the medieval period up to comparatively recently Nuremberg dominated the wooden toy industry and even as early as the 18th century set up export agents in various countries. The Nuremberg merchant produced specifications for toys which were then made in other places but as increasing demand forced up production rates the fine craftsmanship deteriorated. Associated with Nuremberg in the manufacture of wooden dolls were Oberammergau (of festival fame), Berchtesgaden and the Groden Valley. In this country wooden dolls were, in the 18th and 19th centuries, called Dutch dolls; Dutch is a corruption of Deutsch and refers to their German origin.

The early toys were wood (or sometimes clay) but during the middle of the 18th century, wax and composition (mixture of glue and flour) dolls were being made. After the Napoleonic Wars papier mâché came into use and more recently plastic mouldable materials of various kinds.

The doll which played a music instrument, or performed some kind of complicated action was developed and probably reached its peak of perfection during the 18th century. Watchmakers devised intricate clockwork mechanisms driving cog-wheels, cams and cranks to make the doll move and perform to the wonder of all the onlookers.

The subject of mechanical dolls has inspired writers and musicians to produce opera and ballet. *The Tales of Hoffmann* and the ballets *Coppelia* and *Petrushka* are well known to all music lovers. Beside the doll can be ranked toy soldiers and puppets. Punch and Judy shows have delighted children for many years and nowadays the modern equivalent, the TV puppet shows, use dolls which range from the simple glove puppets to the very sophisticated automatons controlled by radio.

Here we have a topic which interests nearly everybody everywhere and which because of its universality can provide common starting points for different children.

Dolls that children bring to school range from crude peg dolls to daintily dressed period costume dolls, and in complexity of construction from solid immovable limbed dolls to those which walk, talk, move their eyes and have fully jointed arms and legs.

4.2 Some teachers' views

Many teachers commented that dolls were rather static, they did not *do* anything. Consequently dolls were mainly used as starting points and quite often the project did not begin to lift off until it had generated enough interest away from the doll itself. Once again it is useful to note that on the whole teachers had to supply the initial guidance. Science discovery did not just happen, it arose through the skill of the teacher; as one teacher put it: 'Really one of the secrets of this kind of work is getting the children to see that their line of enquiry aims not so much at finding the answer, but to see what happens, and helping them to develop this sense of curiosity, with the teacher on the spot to guide them and encourage them in difficulties.'

One teacher found that her class 'were hooked on soft toys' and wondered why.

4.3 Dolls which have been used in school

The following is a summary of some of the work which was carried out by children between the ages of five and eleven.

4.3.1 Action Man diver*
This was used by a teacher of five-year-olds who wrote '. . . an excellent toy for this purpose as so many lines of enquiry can follow its initial use'. The work developed along these lines:

i. 'Heavy' things sink in water—'light' things float. What things will sink, what things will float?   1.42, 1.53, 1.59

ii. Air is lighter than water.   1.4

iii. Weights which sink will float if distributed evenly in a container.

*There are references to Action Man in Coloured things Stages 1 & 2.

iv. Wet objects are heavier than when they are dry. How heavy are wet socks compared with dry socks?   1.43

v. Objects are lighter when weighed in water. Feel the weight of the doll in and out of the water. Are they the same? Tie a brick on a length of string and attach to spring balance. Watch what happens when the brick is lowered into a bucket of water   1.28, 2.34

Examples of questions and answers and activity.

a.   Why do air bubbles come to the surface of the water?

Oliver   Because air just won't stay in water.
Andrew   Because air must be lighter than water: because all light things go up and heavy things go down.

b. Can you trap air under water?
Timothy took a glass jar, blew air into it and plunged it into water. After a group had experimented with jars they found air was already in the jar; they did not need to blow into it.

c. When finding things that would float and things that would sink, Alexander said 'Isn't it funny if there was no water all of these things would fall to the ground.' When asked why, he said 'Well I suppose they can't fall any further.'

d. When weighing things in water the children were amazed at their discoveries and Theresa said, 'I bet it wouldn't happen with a great big stone!' We found a very heavy stone and she was astonished to find it was 2 lb lighter in water.

4.3.2. Dolls compared with humans
One line of development was to use the inertness of a doll and to contrast it with the movement of a human body. This was started in a girls' PE lesson and led on to a simple study of the human body. Quite often dolls provided the starting point for simple physiology and related topics (eg a study of

lungs led to air, and eyes to light and colour).

Looking at eye colours.   1.12, 1.52

What eye colours do the children in your class have ?   1.73

How many children fall into each group ?

Make a histogram (or block graph) showing the colour distribution.   1.74

Looking at sizes.

What is the average height of the girls in your class ?

What is the average size of boys ?   2.72

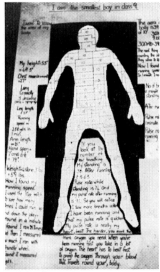 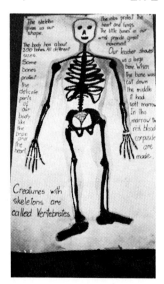

Children's work

4.3.3 Ventriloquist's doll: a doll used as a starting point
A ventriloquist's doll was investigated by a mixed class of nine- and ten-year-old children who decided to find out about their own voices and how sound is produced, travels and is heard.

How can we make a sound ? What is the difference between a noise and a note ? What notes when

played together make a pleasant sound ? How can we make different notes ? What simple musical instruments can we make ? What is an echo ? How far away can we hear the sound made by a penny dropping on to the floor ? Can some children hear better than others ? How can we make sure that we are ' fair ' in our tests ? How can we express our findings ?
1.55, 1.63, 1.04, 1.41. 1.42, 1.44

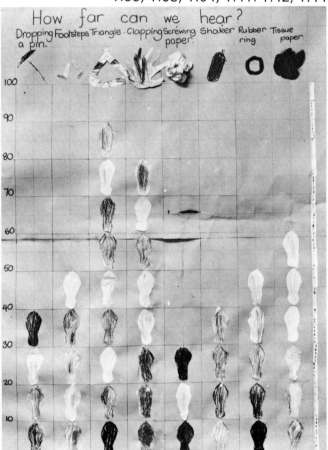

How far away can I hear it ?

Will sound travel through water, metal pipes, a wooden plank ? How fast does sound travel ? Thunder and lightning shows sound to move much slower than light. We need to make a noise and at the same time be seen making the noise. Sound travels fast, approximately 300 m/s (1000 ft/s), so

26

the maker of the noise will have to be a long way from the observer for the sight and sound to be separated by a measurable period of time. Thunderflash fireworks and starter pistols are useful, given suitable safety precautions. One secondary school determined the velocity of sound by observations made on rock blasting and found that the velocity depended upon the wind strength and direction. 2.53, 2.56, 2.42

Once again, sound is a topic for everyone. It can be a very simple one for young children or children in Stage 1, or it can become progressively more and more difficult as children develop. Take the making of sounds. This involves a conversion of one type of energy into sound energy. At first there are simple mechanical conversions, eg handclapping; at the other end of the scale there are more sophisticated conversions, eg chemical energy to sound in the explosion of a cap pistol, or electrical energy to sound in a radio.

4.3.4 A scientific doll
This work was developed by children of eight to ten years old. It started by children bringing their own toys to school and a discussion was initiated by the teacher on the structure and form of movement where appropriate.

Compare this doll with the pop-up man shown in 2.5—what is the connection between the two? How can we make a teapot or a vase less likely to fall over (be more stable)?

Why does the lightweight doll balance on the tight-rope?

The teacher remarked, ' the children appeared to be well satisfied to admire their own and others' toys without wishing to know more. . .'. However, the teacher was not discouraged and brought to school a doll with swinging body and head; this ultimately led to balancing figures * and a tight-rope-walking clown. 1.05, 1.28

---

*See Early experiences.

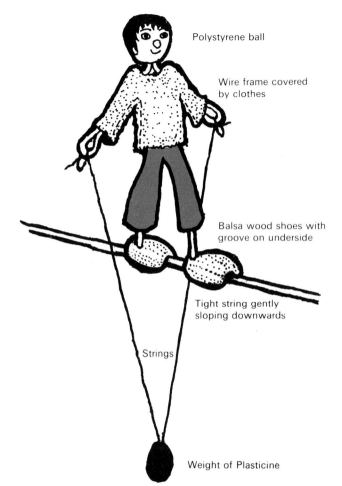

Polystyrene ball

Wire frame covered by clothes

Balsa wood shoes with groove on underside

Tight string gently sloping downwards

Strings

Weight of Plasticine

Why does the light weight doll balance on the tightrope

Various ways of making the clown move down the string were tried. The string was greased but this was unsuccessful because the model moved too quickly. At last a violin bow was used and the string bowed: this produced a gentle vibration and the clown slowly moved down the string. This led to general work on movement and children began to branch out in different directions—the toy had served its purpose.

Further work could have been carried out to find out more about the conditions for balancing: how heavy must the Plasticine be? does the position of the Plasticine matter? 2.34, 1.52

A simple balancing toy made from corks, wire and Plasticine. The toy balances because the centre of gravity (the point through which the weight appears to act) is below the point of support. Children could try the effect of raising the blobs of Plasticine. Does the toy still balance? What is the effect of reducing or increasing the weight of Plasticine?

4.4 Summary: dolls in the classroom

Use	Examples
1. as illustrative material (realism essential)	i. dioramas, Christmas cribs ii. anatomy and elementary physiology iii. armour, dresses iv. ethnological (clothes in other countries)
2. as starting points	i. making things for dolls (dresses, dolls' house) ii. measurements of body sizes iii. sound iv. elementary physiology, looking at ourselves v. movement vi. materials (what is the doll made of?) vii. art, craft, creative writing, making dolls viii. balancing
3. dolls used as such for a purpose	i. puppets and toy theatre ii. gravity toys—the pop-up dolls

In some schools, once the start was made, the work expanded into an enormous variety of topics, each group of children pursuing their own interest. The work of one London school on a dolls' house is illustrated by the chart on page 32.

5 Dolls' house

Photograph of a doll's house exhibited by the Bethnal Green Museum; questions relating to this toy are given on the opposite page

5.1 Introduction

In some museums, dolls' houses can be found dating back to the 17th century. Sometimes these were intended to instruct the children of well-to-do parents of their tasks and responsibilities when they grew up; sometimes the house itself was a builder-architect's model built for some prospective client.

Today many of these old dolls' houses reveal the modes and patterns of past ages and as such are useful to anyone interested in history. The Bethnal Green Museum in London has a number of dolls' houses and a pamphlet is issued giving some details and asking questions which the children can only answer if they look very carefully at the exhibits. Such a technique could be used for your school visits.

A dolls' house can provide starting points even though it is so static, and if unfurnished it might even prove to be a challenge as two girls of ten found when they wanted to wire their dolls' house with electric light. They made their switches from drawing pins and paper-clips.*

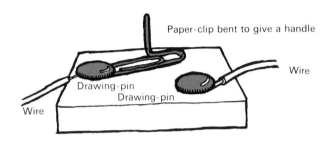

Paper-clip bent to give a handle

Wire

Drawing-pin
Drawing-pin

Wire

A very simple on-off switch which remains on when switched on

*See Early experiences.

3.   This house was built in 1760. It came from Dorset and belonged to a family called Tate. It may have been a copy of their own house made by the Estate Carpenter, but it is anyway a small version of an elegant eighteenth century house. No longer a box divided into four, it is like a real house with a basement, fine flights of steps leading up to the front door and through this an entrance hall and main staircase leading up to the bedrooms.

–   What other things do you see that make this house more like a real home?

–   How did they heat this house?

–   Draw the front of another eighteenth century dolls' house on this gallery which is like a real house in miniature.

5.2 Investigations which might be encouraged

5.2.1 Furnishing a dolls' house*
If the house is unfurnished then quite a lot can be done in decorating, colour schemes and making simple furniture. 'The children enjoy being "grown up" as they design their own house and decide on their own choice of furniture.' Another comment was, 'The children were surprised to find out how much it cost to furnish a real house. The house could be wired for electric light. They would have to know about parallel and series circuits or find out using simple apparatus.

1.17, 1.56, 2.53, 2.58

5.2.2 Working with a dolls' house
The dolls' house can be used as a starting point for : drawings and plans, towards the real thing, patterns, practical uses, making a dolls' house, structures and simple electricity.

Drawings and plans
Drawings and plans involving measurements, scale plans—first of all full size then different scales.

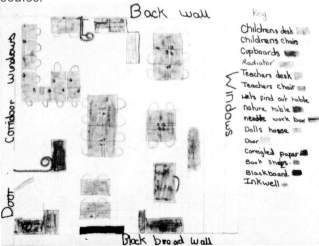

The plan of our classroom

*See Coloured things, 'Home colours'.

One teacher said, 'Most children (girls aged nine to ten) found difficulty with the bird's-eye view. The door also caused a problem.'

1.74, 1.77, 1.91, 2.26

Towards the real thing
They could relate the dolls' house to their own homes and consider services such as water, gas, electricity, telephones, drains, garbage-disposal. 'The children found the story of water fascinating. Most had no idea how water reached their homes, it was just accepted that it should be there. Several experiments have been suggested by children to show how much water is used by a family in one day.' Simple electrical circuits are generally very interesting to children even in the infant classes,† particularly if there is a purpose such as learning about the lights in their own home. (A warning about mains voltage might be appropriate).‡

1.56, 1.76, 1.58, 2.85, 2.53

Patterns
The brickwork of a wall makes a pattern. How many different patterns can they find out? Suppose they examine walls of houses, what can they find out? Are all the patterns the same? What is bonding? What different types of bonding are there? Make some model bricks to scale from balsa wood and use them to show how a wall is built. What happens to the bricks above a window? Why don't they fall down? What is the size of a brick? Are all bricks the same size and shape? What is the colour? Where are they made? How are they made? How much does a brick weigh? Does it weigh more if it is wet? What is this dark strip near the bottom of the wall? How is an arch built? § Why do some bricks have a 'bit pushed in' or have holes in them. Could we build a wall with bricks of other shapes?

1.24, 2.34, 2.52, 1.77, 2.74, 2.54, 2.46

These are a few of the questions which arose

†See Early experiences, 'Doing things'.
‡ See Safety at School, DES pamphlet no. 53, pp 12-14.
§See Structures and forces, Stages 1 & 2.

from a class of children who had become interested in building by looking at a toy house.

Such interest could be guided into looking at civil engineering or architecture or even into historical buildings. In some regions local 2.85 building materials and methods might be studied and contrasted with those elsewhere. The thatched roof and cob walls of a Devonshire cottage contrast with the slates and stone of a Lake District house, or the brick and tiles of London. It is worthwhile keeping alive the knowledge and traditions of our regions—they are so diverse and while it is difficult to frame a precise behavioural objective for an appreciation of customs, regional differences and architecture which fits into a landscape, it is still worthwhile to have such ideas in mind. No one built a dwelling place with aesthetic considerations as the only factor. The cob walls of Devon made for cottages which were warm in winter and cool in summer: why? The slates and stone of the Lake District stand up to the driving rains of one of our wettest regions. Why is London largely built of brick?

Practical uses

It might be worthwhile to interest children in the practical use of models. Cars are designed from models which are often built around figures of the 'average man and woman'. When one school laboratory was designed the teacher concerned made scale models of benches, pupils, stools and the four walls and then juggled the pieces until an acceptable design was obtained. Cupboards and shelving were added so that they were conveniently placed. Such a model enabled the designer to make sure that there was enough working space, that pupils did not keep having to cross one another's paths to fetch things, and that there was no wasted space. Children might like to design kitchens and other rooms this way. In one school, children constructed models and put them together to make a 'City of the Future'.

2.11, 2.74, 2.46

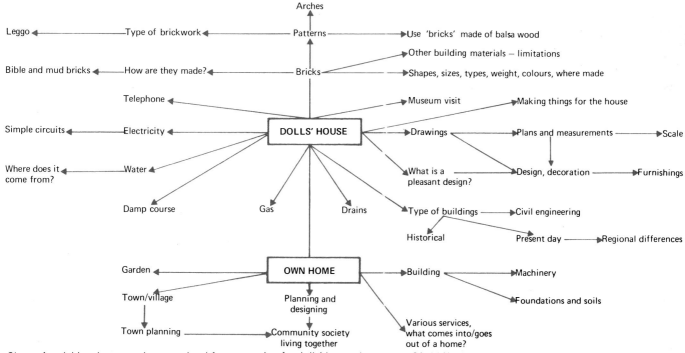

Chart of activities that arose in one school from a study of a dolls' house (age range $8\frac{1}{2}$-$10\frac{1}{2}$)

Construct a model of your classroom, your school, your town. This would provide endless opportunities for exercising ingenuity, observation, measurement, working to scale, practical work and art-work.

Making a dolls' house

Some children made their own dolls' house at school using polystyrene ceiling tiles. This was a highly successful venture because not only did they design, decorate and furnish the house but they also learnt something about glues * and polystyrene. At first they used model cement and found that it made big holes in the tiles. This prompted them to investigate the action of different glues on the tiles and so find one which was satisfactory.

Structures

Much of the structural work arising from a consideration of the building of a house is dealt with in the Unit *Structures and forces Stages 1 & 2.*

Simple electricity

A doll's house presents an excellent opportunity to introduce simple electricity. 'How can we put lights in the house?' Simple circuits are given in 5.3.

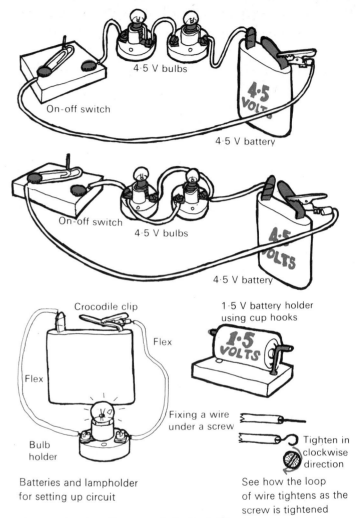

On-off switch

4·5 V bulbs

4·5 V battery

On-off switch

4·5 V bulbs

4·5 V battery

Crocodile clip

Flex

Flex

Bulb holder

Batteries and lampholder for setting up circuit

1·5 V battery holder using cup hooks

Fixing a wire under a screw

Tighten in clockwise direction

See how the loop of wire tightens as the screw is tightened

5.3 Background information for teachers

5.3.1 Simple circuits

The bulbs will light only dimly in a series circuit.

Now try two 2·5 V-bulbs. What do you notice?

The bulbs both light brightly in a parallel circuit.

There is a circuit which is used for switching a light on or off at two different places, eg at the top and bottom of a flight of stairs. The circuit is

shown in the diagram labelled 'Two-way switching circuit'.

5.3.2 Simple switches (see 5.1 and 10.12)

A bulb connected to a battery will remain alight only if there is a complete circuit from one battery terminal to the other. If the circuit is broken the bulb will go out. Breaking the circuit is done by using a simple on-off switch.

But note some children have connected an on-off switch across (in parallel with) a bulb; this is undesirable.

---

* *Gloy Schools Service issue a pamphlet on pastes and glues (cf 11.3); Model and Allied Publications Ltd publish a short book on adhesives (cf 11.2).*

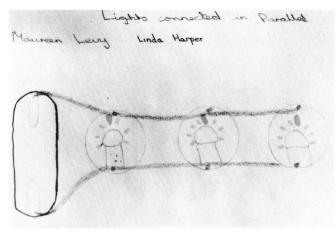

Bulbs in parallel – lighting three bulbs from the same battery

When the switch is *switched on* the bulb goes out ; this is because the switch short circuits the battery and the electric current mainly flows through the switch not the bulb. Short circuited batteries run down very quickly and may in some cases damage the switch or wiring. If at any time the electric mains is short circuited in such a way, the fuses will blow and there is a likelihood of an explosion or a fire.

5.3.3 Two-way switching
This is used in halls and stairways so that a light can be switched on and off from two places, eg at the top and foot of a flight of stairs.

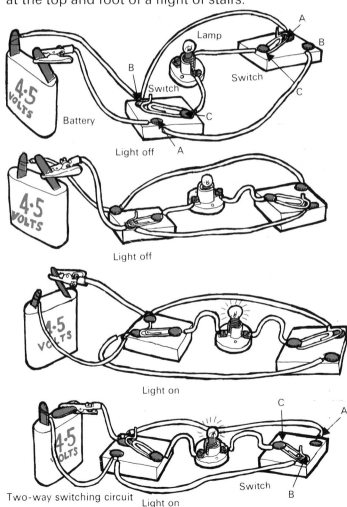

Light off

Light off

Light on

Two-way switching circuit   Light on

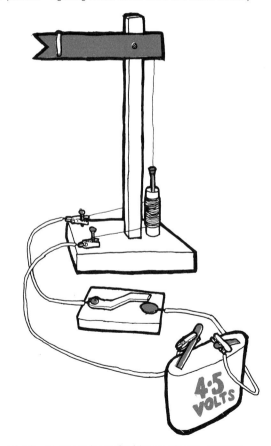

This model railway signal is worked by an electro-magnet
The circuit and switch for the railway signal

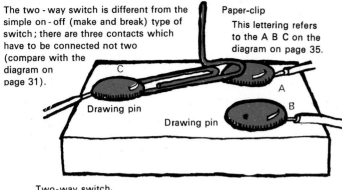

The two-way switch is different from the simple on-off (make and break) type of switch; there are three contacts which have to be connected not two (compare with the diagram on page 31).

Paper-clip
This lettering refers to the A B C on the diagram on page 35.

C

A

B

Drawing pin

Drawing pin

Two-way switch·

Two-way switching is too advanced for most children but it may be that the bright ones may question how it is possible to switch on and off their lights from two places (eg light in bedrooms, corridors, stairs).

5.4 Some possible objectives

Awareness of the structure and form of living things. 1.26

Appreciation of the need for measurement. 1.43

Development of a concept of environment. 1.82

5.4.1 Stage 1
When making furniture for a dolls' house children need to have ideas of the proportions of their bodies in relation to things around them, otherwise the scale of everything will be astray. Chairs with seats on a level with tables indicate that they lack an appreciation of how the pieces of their environment fit together. This is on a far more practical level than the distortions found in paintings and drawings and can be helped by actual constructional work using balsa wood or polystyrene tiles. Measurements are needed when making plans and models.

Awareness of sources of heat, light, electricity, water and gas. 1.56

Although the first three are common energy sources and are found stated in objective 1.56 the other two are included because they too are common services. Teachers have reported that children accept these types of services as being there without wondering why. They often accept the inevitability of common objects and events without question. *

Aesthetic awareness.

Although it is difficult to define aesthetic awareness as an objective, we instinctively (intuitively?) know what we are trying to achieve. We are trying to build up a colour sense, a sense of balancing shapes, a sense of proportion; the often indefinable which is the key to great art. Many scientists consider that a scientific creation has a similar aesthetic quality comparable to a painting or a great piece of poetry. On the other hand artists often make use of scientific materials and methods.

Appreciation that properties of materials influence their use. 1.92

During the construction of a dolls' house useful discussions could be held as to why a particular material is used for a certain purpose. At first, this could be on a very elementary level, eg the impracticability of a gingerbread house *(Hansel and Gretel)*, but with increased ability or age more advanced ideas could be introduced—copper wires for electric light, plastic or lead for waste pipes, the painting of wood and metal window frames. It is always a question of why, why, why?

5.4.2 Stage 2
Ability to visualise objects from different angles.

This ability is needed in order to draw plans and diagrams accurately without help. A dolls' house which comes to pieces is useful for children to check their drawing. 'Is it right?' Look at your door and look at the door in the dolls' house. This objective is an extension of *awareness that the*

See teachers' comments, 4.2, 4.34.

apparent size, shape and relationships of things depend on the position of the observer. 1.91

Interest in the way discoveries were made in the past. 2.13

Awareness of some discoveries and inventions by famous scientists. 2.55

When the dolls' house is related to the real world there are a number of men and inventions which could be studied. Who were the pioneers of gas and electricity ? Who invented the electric light bulb ? or (if we look at inventions without an inventor) when did we first have chimneys or window glass ? Why were the old glass windows made up of a number of small pieces of glass leaded together ? How have the table and chair evolved ? What is glass ? How is a bottle made ? These are a few of the questions I have been asked by children. *

Knowledge of sources and simple properties of common forms of energy. 2.53

This implies that there is a recognition that the go of things (energy), has many forms and can be changed from one form to another. We are doing this constantly in a home. We use fuel in various ways, turn on the electricity to get light and heat,

---

* *The Geffrye Museum in London has a number of rooms furnished with period furniture and fittings. Is there a suitable museum near you ?*

and the radio or TV, or vacuum the carpet. The 'fridge, sewing machine, food mixer, electric drill and hair dryer, all contain motors which require energy to make them go. This they get from the electricity mains.

Awareness of the change in the physical environment brought about by man's activity. 2.85

Most of us live in an urban society : children grow up to accept the world around them ; to them milk comes from bottles, not cows. They need to be made aware of what we are doing to our environment ; whether it is by piling up industrial wastes on some tip in a Welsh valley or a Midland moor, or by constructing a hydroelectric system in the Highlands of Scotland. They also need to look at what is happening on their own doorsteps ; at the rows of houses and towering blocks of flats. Let them make models of towns and plan the services and the roads. Where would they put the factories ? or the Schools ?
The dolls' house is an island community, let us try and get the children to imagine a host of dolls' houses, a wider community, and so go from the particular to the general.

Appreciation of reasons for safety regulations. 2.03

Safety regulations need explaining. They are training in essential habits. The layout of a model community needs thought about road safety : the use of tools requires the conscious adoption of elementary safety rules.

6 Boats (Stages 1, 2 and 3)

'Nice? It's the only thing', said the Water Rat solemnly, as he leant forward for his stroke. 'Believe me, my young friend, there is nothing—absolutely nothing—half so much worth doing as simply messing about in boats.'
(*The Wind in the Willows.* Kenneth Grahame)

6.1 Introduction

Water has a powerful attraction for children. The sea-side, boats, water pistols or simply splashing about (but not always washing) seem to attract and amuse children, and at an early age small boats in the bath are common-place.

What keeps a boat up? Why have a keel? How do sails work? Questions like these, and many more, may occur to adults but often the child is likely to accept the workings of the world around him—it just happens. Frequently children need to be made aware that there are questions to be asked and problems to be solved, and it is our task to be there; to ask and perhaps to prompt and above all to be an organiser of resources. *

6.2 Background information for teachers

6.2.1 Methods of propulsion
wind	electricity
steam	diesel engines
Jet X	clockwork.
elastic	

* *See teachers' comments 4.2, 4.34 and 5.41.*

6.2.2 How do sails work?
If you have ever watched dinghies racing you will have noticed that boats not only sail with the wind behind them (astern) or on the side (a beam) but also they sail into the wind. The old square rigged boats could not use their square sails to sail into the wind; with sails such as these they could only 'drive before the wind'.

Look at the flags at the masthead of the yachts; these show that the yachts are heading into the wind

However, with the development of the 'fore and aft rigged' boat, sailors found that they were able to point the boat into the wind. How is it that a boat can sail into the wind? To understand how this is so, we must look at an aeroplane wing— why doesn't an aeroplane fall out of the sky? For an aeroplane to stay up air must be moving across its wings when the weight of the aircraft is supported mainly due to a suction (lift) which exists above its wings.

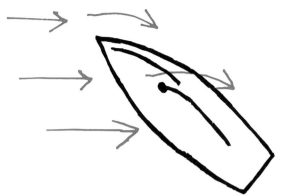

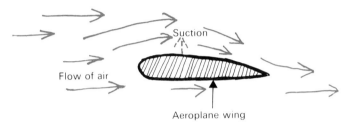

This lift can be shown if a piece of thin paper is held as shown in the diagram and then air is blown over the top surface—what happens to the paper?

This moving air causes a suction on the sheltered (lee) side of the sails and so the boat heads into the wind. However, the suction force is not straight ahead but is somewhat to one side.

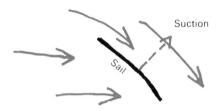

To prevent the boat going sideways it has a keel (see page 43) which serves it in two ways:

i. preventing sideways movement

ii. helping to keep the boat upright (see page 43).

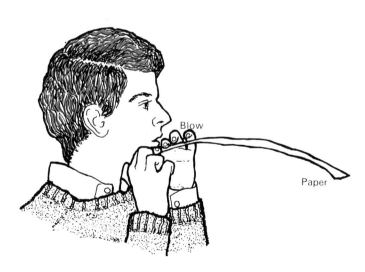

When a sailing dinghy heads into the wind the air moves over the sails.

Most (but not all) fore and aft boats have more than one sail and when heading into the wind the sails ahead of the mainsail channel the wind so that it flows smoothly over the mainsail. If the air flow is not smooth then the sail loses 'lift' and the mainsail may start to flutter. Exactly the same thing can happen to an aeroplane and then the wing is said to stall.

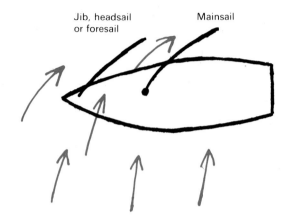

A British aircraft firm, Handley Page, introduced a device (slots) for aircraft wings which works on the same principle as a jib sail and enables planes to land at a much lower speed without stalling. The Messerschmitt 163 produced during World War II, incorporated slots into the leading edges of the wings so making the plane virtually impossible to stall.

6.2.3. Jet X motors
Jet X units bought from model shops are really small rechargeable rockets powered by a chemical (guanidine nitrate) which when lit decomposes giving off heat and large volumes of gases. These gases are squirted out of a small hole and provide the thrust. The unit can be mounted in a small clip and used to drive boats, cars or aircraft : they provide useful propulsion units. The motors provide excellent examples of rocket propulsion and could be used to illustrate work which arises on space and rockets. However, the thrust generated is insufficient to lift the Jet X's own weight so that it cannot be used to propel a home-made rocket ship, but it can be (and has been) used for driving boats, small captive cars (attached to fishing line and a central pillar) and small balsa aircraft.

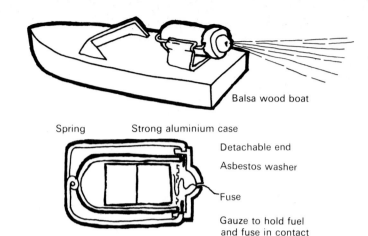

A balsa wood boat powered by a Jet X motor

6.2.4. Elastic motors
Different sizes of propeller should be made and tested to find the best size for the job. Each propeller should be tested with different amounts of twist (pitch) to find the best pitch for a given size of propeller.

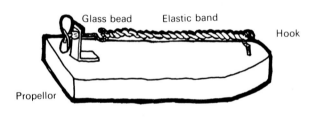

Balsa wood boat powered by a rubber band

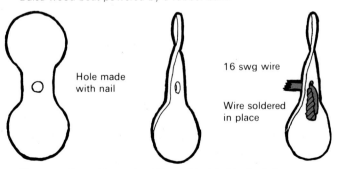

The propeller cut from sheet tin and twisted to form the propeller shape

6.2.5 Electric, diesel and steam propulsion units

These are more complicated but there are 'kits' which can be made up although they are usually rather expensive.

6.3 Testing boats

6.3.1 Speed

I suppose one of the most powerful motivation forces is, 'How can I make my boat go faster than John's?' This involves testing and could lead to a development programme. The problem then becomes one of devising how the testing could be carried out. In boats there are two main factors influencing the speed: i. the hull design, ii. the method of propulsion.

Hull design and streamlining tests *can* be carried out in the classroom. What we need to do is to measure how long it takes for a boat to go a measured distance when propelled by a fixed force. The need for this can be established during discussions. How can we construct a stretch of water in a classroom? A length of plastics or aluminium guttering makes a good test tank: the ends need blocking off but 'end pieces' can be bought. The fixed force can be due to a weight attached to a length of thread running over a pulley.   2.92, 2.46, 2.35

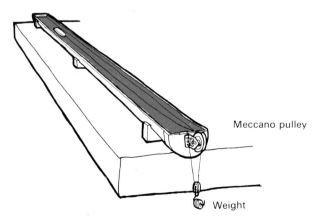

Apparatus for measuring the effect on speed of streamlining

Without a pulley system, the boat is towed the same distance as the weight falls. So there is no point in having a longer length of guttering than about 1m, because the height of the table will not allow the weight to fall any further. (If a pulley system were used the length of the tank could be extended: the boat would travel twice as far and twice as fast as the weight.)

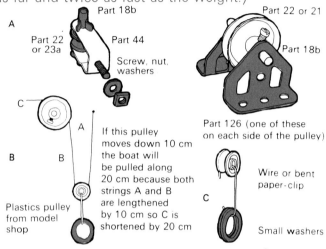

(a) Meccano pulleys for the apparatus to be fitted to the end of the guttering.
(b) How the pulley system is put together and how it works.
(c) Fitting the plastics pulley.

This apparatus can be designed by children provided the teacher knows what will work and can ask leading questions. Streamline flow can be studied by dropping small drops of ink or sawdust ahead of the boat as it is being towed along the tank. The apparatus can be used for quite a number of investigations, for example: 2.46   2.58

i. effect on speed of shapes of boats   2.35

ii. effect on speed of sizes of boats   2.41

iii. effect of altering the towing force   2.42

iv. for small boats does painting and smoothing have any noticeable effect on speed?

v. effect on speed of adding a detergent to the water to make it more slippery.   2.72

One school investigated the waves made by the boat when it was towed through the water. The children recorded their observations by pasting a cut-out piece of white paper representing the hull on to a sheet of black paper and then using string to indicate the waves.

The pulley system at the end of the guttering

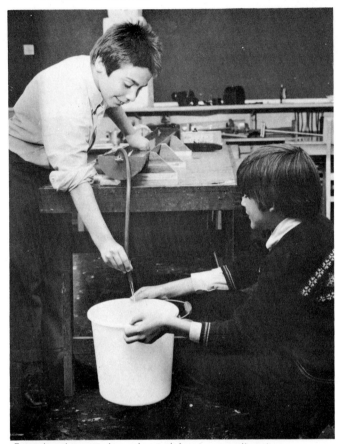

Using plastics guttering as a testing tank for small boats

Emptying the guttering using à siphon — up-ending the guttering causes a flood

Studying the wake formed in the water by towing a hull made of expanded polystyrene

Discussing the results of an investigation is a very important part of the work

6.3.2 Stability

It is all very well having a fast hull but not much good if it is not stable and capsizes in a 'capfull' of wind. With sailing yachts this is most important and here the depth of keel and the weight on the bottom of it have an effect on stability. How could this stability be measured?

One school tried by seeing how much sideways force was needed on the top of the mast to make the boat capsize. Of course, all boats cannot have the same height of mast and the hull and keel may be of different designs. We must be fair, but how? Here we have a situation in which there are a number of variables which need sorting out. What are these variables? A complete list is a formidable one but the following are likely to be the relevant ones. (Not all of them can be effectively investigated by children.)

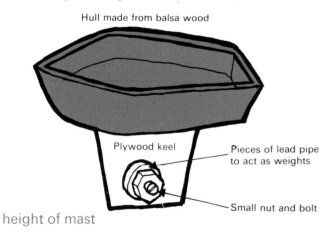

Hull made from balsa wood

Plywood keel

Pieces of lead pipe to act as weights

Small nut and bolt

height of mast

depth of keel

weight of keel and the point through which the weight acts (centre of gravity)
force of wind on sails, which will depend upon the area of sails and the height of the sails above the water line.
(Have you ever thought what are the advantages of having a sail shaped like a right-angled triangle or why the sails on a wind-jammer become smaller towards the tops of the masts?)

beam (width) of the boat   2.42

Some children looked at catamarans and compared their stability with conventional boats (see 6.54).

Pitching

Rolling

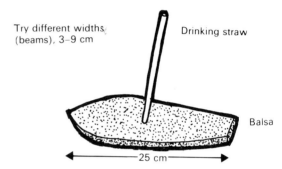

Try different widths (beams), 3–9 cm

Drinking straw

Balsa

25 cm

Boats pitch and roll. How does the shape of the boat influence pitching and rolling? Try boats which are narrow and those which are broad: which rolls least? Does the keel have any effect on rolling? Does the length of the boat influence the pitching?   2.43, 2.92, 2.11

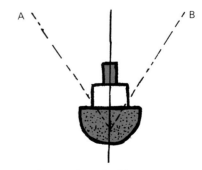

A   B

The boat rolls from *A* to *B*. How can we measure the rolling? This could be an opportunity to introduce parts of a circle and on to degrees.   2.44

6.4 Flotation

I suppose for anyone who has taken science, even those who have had only a smattering, this will evoke Archimedes' Principle and grim memories of displacement lightened perhaps with stories of golden crowns and bath tubs. To understand Archimedes' Principle and flotation requires an acceptance of the concept of volume conservation. One grammar school carried out tests on its first-year pupils to see whether they were ready to profit from a study of Archimedes' Principle to explore flotation. It was found that up to forty per cent of the pupils were not sure about conservation of volume so that for them displacement cans and the like would be a matter of learning by rote and not based on understanding.

At an early stage children might come to realise that solid lumps of some materials float whereas solid lumps of other substances sink. Let us make a suitable record of those things which will float and those that will sink. Later children may realise that whereas iron *ships* float, a poker will sink. The simplest explanation is that an iron ship is not all iron but a mixture of air which floats and iron which sinks and it is the air which 'wins'. A tin can may float but fill it with something like sand which displaces the air and is heavier than water and it will sink. A metal milk top can be made to float like a boat but screwed up it will sink.

2.92, 2.33, 1.59, 1.44, 1.42

6.5 Investigations which might be encouraged

Shapes and streamlining—formation of waves

Use of sails—rather depends on local stretch of water but some work can be done indoors using a fan

Other forms of propulsion

Function of the keel

Multi-hulled ships

Reading about actual voyages of discovery and round-the-world sailing—transatlantic race, tall ships race, tea clippers, *Cutty Sark*

Mechanical systems

6.5.1 Shapes and streamlining
What shape goes through the water the fastest?
2.41

If you double the force driving a boat do you double its speed? 2.26, 2.24, 2.72

What are the shapes of a racing canoe? 2.42 a destroyer? a rowing boat? a punt? Why are the shapes different?

When a boat moves through the water what waves does it make? Do the shapes and sizes of the waves depend on the shape of the boat?

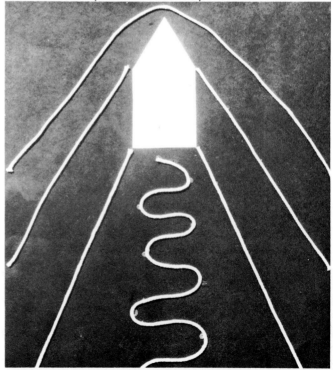

Waves made by a boat, using string and black paper for recording

6.5.2 Sails and keel
Some work could be done with stiff paper sails mounted on a small balsa boat and air blown by an electric fan. Sails could be set in various positions and made of different shapes. Small boats could be fitted with and without keels and the difference noted in their sailing. Does it matter how big the keel is made? The sailing pond could be a plastic bowl, and the wind could come from a small plastic-bladed fan. *   2.42

6.5.3 Other forms of propulsion
What other forms do children know of? Even with steam ships there were paddle-steamers and sternwheelers (Mississippi) beside propeller-driven ships. There are also airscrew-driven boats which are used in the Everglades of Florida, USA. Some of the boats mentioned can be built up in toy form. How do hovercraft work? What are the principles of their hovering and their propulsion? Are they boats? (There is a vacuum cleaner and a lawn mower which work on the hover principle.)   2.58, 2.53, 1.58, 1.28

A simple jet-propelled boat, easy to make, is described in 10.3.

6.5.4 Multi-hulled boats
The catamaran is now well known; children might consider the advantages and disadvantages of such a craft. (It will not easily right when capsized and will not sail close to the wind.) They might contrast the stability of a single-hulled boat with that of a catamaran.

The following is an extract from an article by Mr A. J. Nancollas, Headmaster of Bodsham, CE Primary School, Elmstead, Kent and published in the *Kent Education Gazette*, October, 1968.

'The "angle of overturn" of different kinds of yacht was measured by attaching weights at a series of points on the masts of models in a

---

* *See* Early experiences *for details of making a suitable fan from a model aircraft propeller and a small electric motor run off a 4.5 V battery.*

water tank. The children concluded:

'It seemed to us that the trimaran is more stable than the catamaran and the monohull, as with the weight hung on the 18th pin the trimaran only tilted to 18 degrees, whilst the catamaran tilted to 18 degrees with the weight on the 9th pin. The monohull tilted to 18 degrees when the weight was placed on the 3rd pin. All the boats were more stable when the weight was placed on the lowest pin. The higher the weight was placed the more likely the boat was to overturn. We found little difference in the stability of the monohull when the weight was placed on pins 13–18. We found that if we reduce the height of the mast and increase the area of the keel, the yacht is more stable in the water tank.'

The catamaran is a twin-hull boat

Further work included tests of the strength of different designs and sizes of masts and cross-members, the construction of a model wave to test the reaction of multi-hulls to the crest, side and trough, consideration of the effects of using different materials, forms of boat construction, design of floats and so on, and finally the construction by groups of children of multi-hulls of their own design, using the findings of the preceding work.'

Natives of some South Sea Islands use 'outrigger canoes'. Which is right *A* or *B* ? Children could make small models and find out. 2.46, 2.11

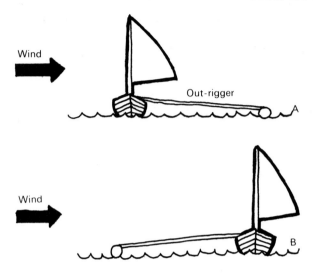

Should the outrigger be to windward or leeward of the boat?

The outrigger is detachable and adjustable

Does this boat require a keel? Can it sail into the wind? Try other shapes of sails. Try altering the position of the mast.

Perhaps a number of children could make identical hulls and outriggers then try various sails and positions of masts according to their own ideas. Then the models could all be raced together. If we do this how can we make sure that we are being fair? 2.43

6.5.5 Mechanical systems
Most toy boats other than sailing yachts use some form of engine. What works the engine? Where does the energy come from? Are there any gear wheels? What do they do? (In a clockwork motor the propeller revolves *faster* than the main

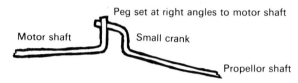

Connection of the motor shaft to the propeller shaft

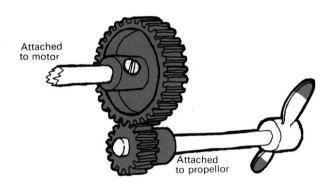

This system speeds up the propeller

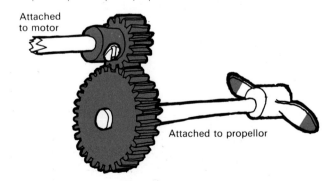

This system slows down the propeller

spindle which is wound up ; in an electric motor boat the propeller revolves either at the same rate as the electric motor or at a slower rate.) How is the motor connected to the propeller ? (Sometimes there is a simple universal joint so the shaft of the motor need not be aligned with propeller shaft. In other toy boats the connection is made by a piece of thin rubber tubing or a piece of curtain spring.) Gear trains (sets of gear wheels) could be set up in Meccano to find out about gearing. There are some good plastic gear wheels sold in model shops.   2.58, 1.64, 2.53, 2.52, 1.58

6.5.6 Tanks and ponds
Boats need water, water must be contained, but how ? What containers are suitable and available ?

i. Plastic bowls, small but suitable for stability investigations.

ii. Metal trays, such as are used in canteens and bakeries about 5 cm deep, used for investigations into sails.

iii. Plastic guttering, can be bought in various widths, the 15 cm is very suitable for investigations into streamlining.

iv. Plastic sheeting, some schools have built in the playground a temporary boating pool from bricks and plastic sheeting (the children also learnt something about bonding because bricks put on top of one another, as in (b), are easily

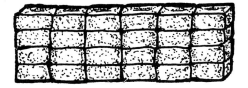

pushed over, whereas those assembled, as in (a), are quite stable). * The size of such a pond only depends on space and materials available and it can be used for more ambitious investigations such as testing model jet-propelled speedboats.

v. Children's plastic paddling pools are fine for work with boats.

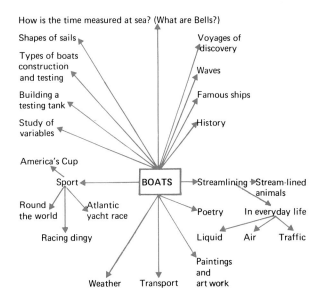

Chart of topics which have arisen from boats (age range 5-13)

6.6 Some possible objectives

6.6.1 Stage 1
Recognition of common shapes—square, circle, triangle.
1.23

Willingness to consider the shape and size of things.

If children look beyond the toy and at the big boats what shapes and sizes do they see ? Do some boats have a characteristic shape ?

* *See* Structures and forces Stage 1 & 2.

Why? Why is a racing canoe long and narrow and a punt broad? Are all cargo ships the same shape?

Ability to use new words appropriately.   1.71

There are hosts of 'new' words associated with ships and the sea. How many are appropriate for children must be left to individual teachers.

Willing compliance with safety regulations in handling tools and equipment.   1.08

Awareness of cause-effect relationships.   1.81

Here is the conscious effort to find out by a planned alteration of conditions and not by haphazard and hopeful changes.

6.6.2 Stage 2
Awareness of symmetry in shapes and structures.
   2.24

A boat is a good example to take to consider symmetry—it has a plane of (mirror) symmetry, but it may contain a host of parts which have a higher degree of symmetry, eg a cylindrical funnel.

Ability to visualise objects from different angles and the shape of cross-sections.   2.26

This objective may be achieved if a child draws a model or attempts to make a simple balsa wood boat. His attention can be drawn to cross-sections and if he is keen and wants to construct a proper model he will need to prepare templates. Details of this type of work can be found in model books.

Appreciation of the reasons for safety regulations.

Appreciation of weight as a downward force.

Familiarity with a wide range of forces and ways in which they can be changed.   2.52, 2.34, 2.03

In considering the stability of a yacht a child has to be able to identify not only the gravitational force but also the force of the wind on the sails

and the water on the keel. It might be pertinent to ask a bright child what it is that stops a boat from going faster and faster. The answer, 'It's the force of the water, sir', really needs looking at more carefully if the child is able. Why does streamlining enable a boat to go faster?

There are at least four factors which combine to 'hold a boat back':

i. the pushing aside of the water,

ii. the pressure of the water against the 'front' (bow) of the boat,

iii. the formation of waves,

iv. friction.

Note. iii. would be absent in a submarine so we should expect submarines to travel fast—they do, and unofficial figures suggest speeds in excess of 40 knots from nuclear submarines.

6.6.3 Stage 3
Awareness of the changes in the physical environment brought about by man's activity.
   2.85, 3.85

Going from the realms of toys to the adult world, what use has man made of boats? (See John Masefield's poems.)

Knowledge that energy can be stored and converted in various ways.   3.52

With mechanical boats we either store energy, eg clockwork motor or elastic motor, or change energy from one form into another, eg with an electric motor, the changes are chemico-electrical to mechanical.

With a diesel motor or steam engine, they are chemical to heat to mechanical. These ideas on energy changes may be difficult for all but the bright child.

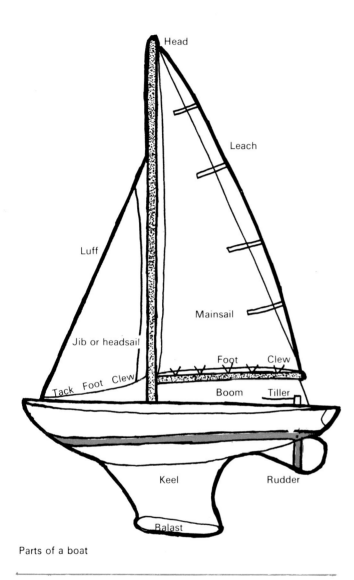

Parts of a boat

iii. expanded polystyrene ceiling tiles, or the material used to pack TV sets, electrical equipment etc, can be cut using a hot wire cutter which can be bought at a decorator's shop

iv. cardboard, sticky tape

v. glue : the most suitable for balsa wood and cardboard is balsa cement as it is quick-drying and waterproof ; for polystyrene use a latex glue or Evo-stik Resin W

vi. thin plywood (1 mm or thereabouts) for cutting out keels

vii. fine sandpaper

viii. model aeroplane varnish

ix. drinking straws

6.7.2 Tools*
balsa wood knife or single edged safety razor blade †

fretsaw, hot wire tile cutter

steel rule

stout board (or an old desk top) on which to cut the wood

G-clamp to hold awkward pieces of wood on the bench hook while cutting them eg holding 1 in square balsa while cutting out the hulls of a catamaran

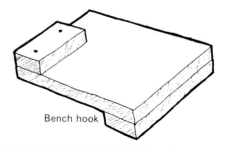

Bench hook

6.7 Building simple boats: practical information

6.7.1 Materials
i. ¼ in (6 mm) balsa wood (the soft variety is easier to cut)

ii. 1 in (25 mm) square soft balsa

---

* See Working with wood Stages 1 & 2.
† Please issue warnings and show how to keep fingers out of the way.

a Surform tool is useful to shape blocks of wood

a small tenon saw should be used to cut wood (other than balsa) in which case the wood should be held in a 'bench hook' to prevent it from slipping

small plane which can be held in the hand

6.7.3 Suitable books
i. *Solarbo Book of Balsa Models,* 75p,
Model and Allied Publications Ltd,
13/35 Bridge Street, Hemel Hempstead, Herts.

ii. *Know your Materials: 208 Adhesives, 209 Balsa, 210 Doping and Finishing, 211 Hardwoods* 30p, MAP Ltd.

iii. MAP publish a number of useful books on specialised aspects of models and handicrafts.

6.7.4 Suitable hulls
i. From cardboard
When stuck together the card needs water-proofing with model aeroplane varnish.

A drinking straw will serve as a mast and this can be 'stepped' in place with a thin piece of card across the boat and a dab of glue at the foot of the straw.

ii. From $\frac{1}{4}$ in (6 mm) sheet balsa
Hulls can be made all shapes and sizes. Simple

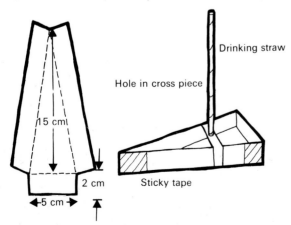

single sheet boats can be used, or more complicated models can be built up using the bread and butter method in which cut-out layers are stuck together and then the outside is smoothed. This way saves the bother of having to carve shapes from solid wood.

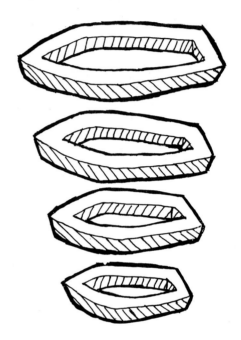

iii. From 1 in (25 mm) square balsa
This material is useful for making small hulls, for catamarans, rolling tests, stability investigations, speed trials. Broader beams can be made by gluing two pieces together. Shaping can be done using a balsa wood knife, razor blade or Surform tool after cutting roughly to shape with a tenon saw.

Note that the saw cuts are not vertical.

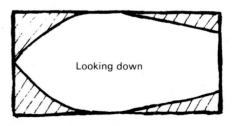

iv. From expanded polystyrene
This material is easily cut with a hot wire cutter (from decorator's shops). *Do not* attempt to sandpaper polystyrene as the dust is considered to be a health hazard. Polystyrene cannot be glued together with balsa cement as the solvent will dissolve it; use a latex glue, Evo-stik Resin W, Lepage's 21 White Glue, Gloy Multiglue.

6.7.5 Finishing
With the exception of polystyrene, all the materials mentioned need sealing with a waterproof varnish, otherwise they will become waterlogged. Model aeroplane varnish is suitable but care needs to be taken to wash out the paint brush in thinners after use otherwise the brush will harden and become useless. Thinners can be purchased from model shops; garages use them for car spraying enamels; chemists can supply acetone which is excellent as a brush cleaner. * All thinners are highly inflammable.

Sealing with aeroplane varnish *must* be done *before* painting *not after*. (On a spare piece of wood try the other way round.)

---

* *If mixed with twenty per cent castor oil, acetone makes a very good nail varnish remover.*

7 Bouncing balls (Stages 1, 2 and 3)

7.1 Introduction

Here we are starting with something every child plays with ; a ball, rubber, tennis, golf, football, all are familiar—so are marbles and ball-bearings. They are thrown, hit, bounced, caught, sat on and even used to keep boats afloat, but the property we are interested in is their bounciness, and this can be investigated at all ages and stages with different degrees of sophistication.

This investigation can be as open-ended or as structured as the teacher considers best for his pupils. The subject can arise naturally, the result of play, or because someone has a ball on his desk and the teacher picks it up and bounces it on the floor. It can continue as an investigation directed by the child aided by the teacher who knows the potentialities, or the teacher may like to prepare work cards of his own. It can be pursued in the secondary school as well as in primary schools.

What can a pupil find out about the bounciness of a ball ? How he tackles this problem will depend upon his age and development. In a simple way he will probably start by dropping the ball and seeing how high it bounces. Then he may go on to relate the height of bounce to the height from which the ball is dropped. Surfaces of various materials and kinds might also be investigated and so on. The teacher can help by asking suitable questions, but, as is so often the case, some knowledge of the background is needed and this is given in the next sections (7.2-7.22).

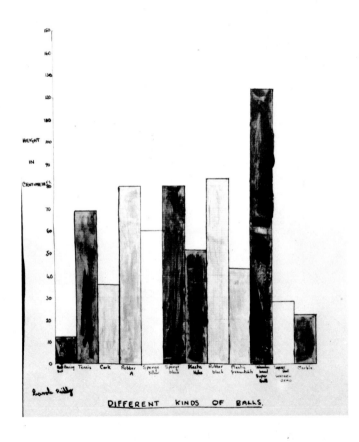

The bouncing of balls ; studying the effect of dropping different balls on to different types of material. The conclusions which can be drawn from these results depend upon the stage of development of the children ; the same results would be meaningful to pupils in the sixth form of a secondary school.

52

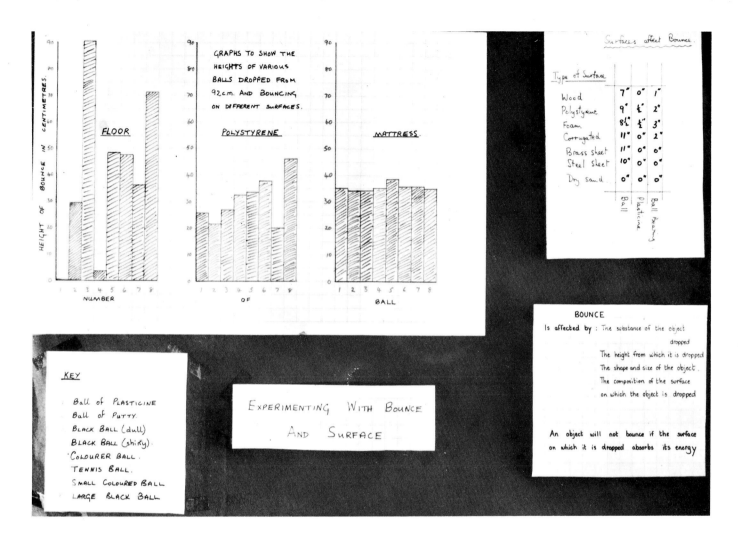

7.2 Background information for teachers

7.2.1 Factors affecting the bouncing of one substance on another

The composition of the ball.

The composition of the bouncing surface (see *Metals Background information*).

Try dropping a ball of Plasticine on the floor and then on an expanded polystyrene ceiling tile.

Does the result suprise you?

The height from which the ball falls.

The cleanness and smoothness of the two surfaces which meet—this will introduce an element of chance.

The rigidity of the surface on which the bouncing takes place, ie whether the surface will rock or is firm and steady.

The reason why substances will bounce is best explained in terms of energy, but only for those children who are ready for such an explanation.

If both ball and bouncing surface are physically the same immediately after the bounce as before, then the ball bounces well. If there is any permanent change, viz the bouncing surface shifting or becoming dented, or if either the ball or surface slowly returns to its original shape, then the bounce will be poorer, because energy has been used up in making a dent or moving the bouncing surface. The shape of the ball influences the bounce (consider soccer and rugby balls).

7.2.2 How energy changes into different forms during the bouncing of a ball-bearing on a piece of metal

A ball-bearing held stationary at A has a certain amount of stored energy (potential energy) which depends on the vertical distance AC.

When the ball-bearing has been released, is falling and has reached position B it has two forms of energy:

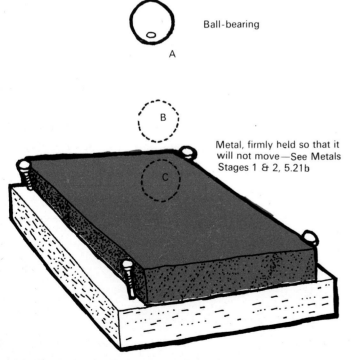

Ball-bearing

A

B

Metal, firmly held so that it will not move—See Metals Stages 1 & 2, 5.21b

C

A ball-bearing held in the air has potential energy

i. that energy which it has owing to its moving (kinetic energy)

ii. that which remains of its stored energy, due to it still having some distance to fall, ie B to C.

Just as the ball-bearing hits the metal all its energy is in the form of moving energy, but then the moving energy is changed into:

i. sound energy—this is lost

ii. heat energy—this also is lost

iii. energy used up in altering the shape of the ball-bearing.

iv. energy used up in altering the shape of the metal.

If sufficient of the energy which is used up in (iii) and (iv) is quickly recovered because the shape is almost immediately completely or partially restored then the ball will bounce. If, however, some of the energy is lost in permanently altering the surface of the metal and/or ball and if the sum of this energy, together with a and b, is equal to the moving energy of the ball just as it hits the metal then the ball will not bounce. All its energy has been used up in sound, heat and altering the shape of the metal and/or the ball. Think what happens when a ball of Plasticine is dropped on to a hard surface. It does not bounce; all the kinetic energy has been used up in producing sound and heat and in altering the shape of the plasticine ball. Sometimes a ball does not bounce very well because it does not return to its original shape quickly enough. It is still returning after it has left the floor.

7.3 Investigations which might be encouraged

7.3.1 Bouncing balls

What can we use?

rubber balls of different types

ball-bearings of different sizes
Plasticine ball
make a collection of different balls   1.05

7.3.2 Surfaces on which to bounce the balls
pieces of wood of different sizes
polystyrene tiles
foam rubber
corrugated paper (use both rough and smooth sides)
metal sheets
small pieces of metal
blocks of metal
dry sand
the floor
[See the Appendix.]

Try dropping a ball from different heights and then plotting height of bounce against height of drop. Is it possible for children to make deductions from such a graph? For example could they predict how high the ball would bounce from a particular height?   1.44, 1.33, 2.42, 1.72, 2.73

As usual in any investigation work the important thing is to get the children interested so that *they* start finding out. The teacher's role is to help and guide; to ask the right questions at the right time and to stimulate discussion. With the background information in 7.2, examples of questions in 7.4, objectives in 7.5 and a flow chart in 7.6 the teacher has an idea of the potentialities of the subject both from subject development and from the inculcation of attitudes and points of view.

Simply dropping a ball and measuring the height to which it bounces provides an opportunity for maths; while the investigation of different surfaces on which to bounce a ball is surely the cue to examine materials.

Dare we suggest that the teacher tries some of the experiments first? There may be some surprising and unexpected results.

7.4 Examples of questions for teacher/pupil

7.4.1 Using a rubber ball
How high does the ball bounce? How can you measure it? How many times does the ball bounce? Does the surface on which you bounce the ball have any effect on the height of the bounce? Does the ball mark the surface?
                                                    1.43, 1.44

Does the ball bounce on sand? Collect a number of rubber balls of different colours and sizes. Do they all bounce to the same height if dropped the same distance?   1.57

How many things can you change to alter the bounce of balls?   2.42, 2.43

7.4.2 Using Plasticine
How high does a ball made of Plasticine bounce when it is dropped on to a block of wood, or a piece of polystyrene tile? Does the shape of the ball alter? (If Plasticine is dropped on to polystyrene or a foam rubber mat, it is the mat which provides the bounce.)

7.4.3 Using a ball-bearing
What substances are you going to drop it on? How high does it bounce? How will you measure it? How could you conveniently prevent the ball-bearing from being lost as it bounces? * Does the nature of the substance on which you carry out the bouncing have any effect on the height of the bounce? Does the size of the bouncing surface have any effect? Is the surface marked? Is there any relationship between the height of bounce and any surface mark which may be produced? Is there an obvious different physical property between a substance on which the ball-bearing bounces well and a substance on which there is a poor bounce? Do big ball-

* *Drop it inside a wide glass tube or a tube made by taping together a strip of transparent plastic film (used for garden cloches) 100 or 90 x 15 cm See Metals Stages 1 & 2, 5.21 b.*

bearings bounce as well as small ones ? If not, why not ? Does the same size ball-bearing always bounce to the same height when dropped on to the same piece of material from a constant height ? If not, why not ?   2.25, 2.42, 2.92, 2.58, 2.41, 2.11

7.4.4 General

Why do substances bounce ? Do balls bounce just as well off a hard substance like iron and off a softer substance like rubber ? (This involves elasticity which is discussed in the background book to *Metals*.) How can you display your observations and results ?

7.5 Some possible objectives which might apply to investigations into bouncing balls

7.5.1 Stage 1
Appreciation of the need for measurement.   1.43

Awareness that more than one variable may be involved in a particular change.   1.44

Ability to tabulate information and use tables. 1.75

Recognition of common shapes—square, circle, triangle.   1.23

Appreciation that ability to move or cause movement requires energy.   1.58

7.5.2 Stage 2
Appreciation of the need to control variables and use control in investigations.   2.43

Ability to investigate variables and to discover effective ones.   2.42

Recognition of role of chance in measurements and experiments.   2.94

Ability to use histograms and simple graphical forms for communicating data.   2.73

7.5.3 Stage 3
Ability to separate, exclude or combine variables in approaching problems.   3.32

Knowledge that energy can be stored and converted in various ways.   3.52

Recognition that energy has many forms and is conserved when it is changed from one form to another.   3.84

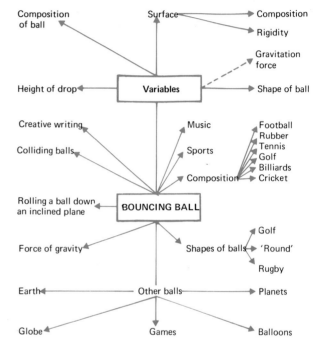

Chart of topics which have arisen from bouncing balls

7.6 An unusual investigation *

A school investigated the bouncing of eggs. They found that if eggs were dropped on their school lawns the eggs bounced unbroken. They arranged for eggs to be dropped from a fireman's ladder and even from an aeroplane and still the majority of the eggs bounced unbroken !

* The children of one school composed, played and taped music which was inspired by bouncing balls of different kinds, eg the pattering of table tennis balls, the thump of a football, the sharp clonk of a golf ball.

The eggs were fresh and not hard boiled, the lawns mown short, but the soil was black alluvium without stones.

7.7 The paths of bouncing balls

If two children *A* and *B* throw a ball to each other so that the ball does not touch the ground, what kind of path does it follow ?

Before they find out ask them to draw what they think the path is. This investigation needs some other children to act as observers.

2.02, 2.05, 2.07, 2.08, 2.94

Now get *A* and *B* to throw the ball so that it bounces at *C*. Once again get the children to make a prediction.

Note: In order that the observers should be able to see clearly the path of the ball get the children to gently lob the ball making it follow the same path each time.

A

B

C

8 Trains and cars

8.1 Introduction

Nearly all boys enjoy playing with toy trains or
car racing sets and if girls are questioned it
emerges that they too would like to have a go if
only their brothers would let them! So we have
something which is popular and which varies in
degrees of complexity to suit all ages (even
Father is ready to play).

Any mechanical toy must have a source of energy.
It must use this energy to do something via
some mechanical system and whatever it does
must be of interest to the operator. Each of these
stages might provide suitable topics for investiga-,
tion but the topic and the depth to which it is
probed will depend upon the interest, maturity
and ability of the pupil involved.

A visitor to one school came upon two boys
during their lunch hour racing model cars around
a track. He stopped and watched. One of the
boys made a comment on the speed of his car
indicating that he thought that it was going at
at least 20 mile/h. The visitor asked him if he
could find out what the speed really was. A lively
argument developed between the two contestants
and some of their supporters and a passing
teacher was drawn into the discussion as referee!
In the end difficulties were sorted out and solved
and the speed of the cars calculated. It proved
to be nearer 2 mile/h rather than the 20 that they
had originally thought. It was not the final result
which was important but rather the solving of
problems which arose.

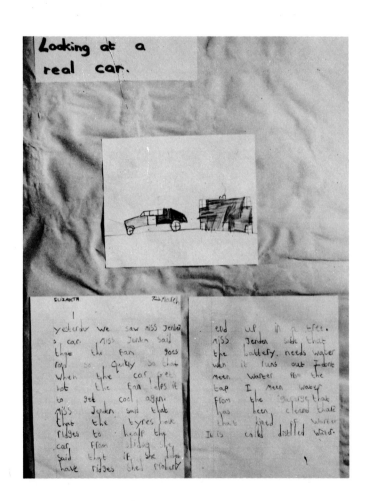

What an infant recorded after looking at teacher's car. It is
interesting to see that these observations on the working of a
car were made by a girl. Girls are interested in mechanical things
if only they are given a chance.

58

8.2 Model railways provide four types of investigation

i. Problems which can be immediately investigated such as speed. How much weight can their trucks carry? How big a slope can the train climb?

ii. Problems which arise from the working of the system. Where does the power come from? How do signals work? What do gears do? How can you alter the speed of the train? How can you make it go backwards? How do you connect the battery? What is a transformer?

iii. Problems which arise when you may want to extend the track or workings: these are usually practical problems. Could a turntable be made? Could some signals be made? Could the track current and the signal be coupled in some way so that the train could only go when the signal was clear?

iv. Investigations which link the model with the real world.

8.3 Investigations and work which might be tried

8.3.1 The immediate problems
Train sets have been tried in a number of schools both in the infant and junior stages. At an early age 'the setting up of the track and manipulation of controls with accuracy needs patience and practice', this alone constitutes valuable training.

It was surprising to find that the same investigations such as speed of the train, effects of loading and slope, were carried out with increasing degrees of sophistication with increasing age; the same type of problem interested children of all ages.

As an example of increased sophistication, a boy of ten suddenly realised that when a car or train

went round a bend different parts of the vehicle went at different speeds. How should the distance around a closed loop be measured? Should it be round the outside rail, the inside rail or doesn't it matter? The actual mechanics of measurement may provide a minor problem especially if there are a number of curves to be investigated. Children might consider the circuits shown. 1.36

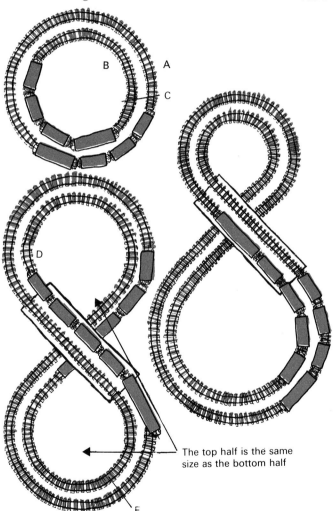

Curved train tracks present problems in measurement of their length

A and B represent two train tracks. If you measure from C all the way around both tracks

59

back to *C,* will the two measurements be the same ?   1.35

D and *E* represent two train tracks which form a figure eight, the crossing being in the form of a bridge. If you measure from *F* all the way round both tracks back to *F* will the two measurements be the same ?   1.43

Suppose the figure eight is not symmetrical ; would the two tracks be of equal length ?   2.24

This type of problem can be investigated by appealing to a sense of 'fairness'—is it fair for one person always to take one track in car racing ? Again the problem might be considered later because although the inside bend will be shorter there will be increased centrifugal forces for the same speed so there will be a greater tendency for the inside car to leave the track. Even this isn't the last word !   1.44

8.3.2 Problems of know-how
These are those which arise from the system, and the natural curiosity of children. What kind of things can a child question and then either work

out or discover for himself ? (Maybe with a little guidance to start him off.) Here are some :

What is the source of energy ? (Battery or mains electricity or clockwork.) What does the control box do ?   1.28, 1.58

What do the gears do ? How many different types of gears can you find ? How does an electric motor work ? This is a tough question and is   2.53 perhaps beyond all but the brightest. How does an electric signal work ? Can we make one ? 3.56 (See page 68.). How does a train go over points ? How do they work ? How are they worked by electricity ?   2.58

What are sparks ? Why does a short-circuit blow a fuse or cause the overload switch to cut out ? A clockwork train could be used to introduce ideas about storing energy.   2.51, 3.52

Maybe there will be an interesting spin off as for example when some girls used cog-wheel motifs to design some lino cuts. In another school cog-wheels formed the basis of a 3-D collage, and in a third school plaster casts were made of cog-wheels and then painted.

8.3.3 Practical problems
These turn up when pupils want to add to the existing layout or alter something. There are problems of inventiveness and making do with the materials to hand. How can we make a bridge or a viaduct ? Can we make our own trucks ? There is a list as long as your arm of things pupils could make to add to their toy. The real question is what use can we make of their enthusiasm ? At first the enthusiasm may almost run wild but gradually it can be channelled so that a modicum of planning is introduced. This is an extremely delicate operation, varying from pupil to pupil. Some children are ready at lower junior age to start thinking about how to do the job, and how to arrange the various stages of some simple construction. Others at a much later age are still in the trial and error era and often find that they cannot finish a job because they have left out a vital stage.

There is no simple panacea but if children work in groups to plan their work then successful practical work, the result of conscious planning, is more likely to develop. Later the more individualistic members could hive off and work on their own so developing their own initiative and inventiveness and becoming self supporting.

8.3.4 From toys to the real thing

There is no reason why we cannot go from the make believe to the real thing and this extension would not need to be confined to scientific aspects but could embrace history and geography, and even art and literature. (Turner's painting *Rain, Steam and Speed: The Great Western Railway*.) The battle between, road, rail and canal forms a part of our social history of the 19th century and today the wheel has turned almost full circle with the closing of local railways. Are there any lines closed down in your district? What takes their place? Are there any narrow gauge railways near you?

How about the history of railways. Who was Brunel?* What was his broad gauge? How are underground tunnels dug? When were electric trains first used? What engines are used now? There is wide interest in railways and enthusiasts have societies, books, films, clubs and even private lines for those who want to know more.

2.85

8.4 Toy cars and slopes

Children love running toy cars down slopes. They might time them over a fixed distance (here is an opportunity for them to design their own timer, eg a water clock) and see how the slope alters the speed and time.   2.58, 1.36, 2.35

They could find out if weights in the toy alter the speed.   1.41

* *See L. T. C. Rolt, Isambard Kingdom Brunel, Longman Group Ltd. This is the first full biography of Brunel to be written since 1870.*

What other clocks can be devised? See *Time* and *Structures and Forces Stages 1 & 2*. When using a clock such as this, it is convenient to have one child counting the drops aloud and even using a count down technique, eg 3, 2, 1, 0 (or start or go), 1, 2, etc.

Squeezy bottle with the end cut off

Nozzle made from Plasticine pierced by a pin and then squeezed until the water just drips

A simple water clock for measuring time in drops

Weigh the car on an elastic band, then use the same band attached to the car as a towing rope and pull it up a slope. Does the band stretch to the same amount in both experiments? Does the amount of slope influence the degree of stretch of elastic band? Why does a road zigzag up a steep hill? What are the advantages of a spiral staircase?   2.52

All sorts of things can be rolled down slopes: model cars, marbles, ball bearings, balls, tins, pieces of pipe

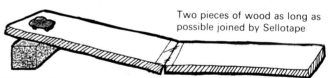

Two pieces of wood as long as possible joined by Sellotape

This length can be raised so that a shallow V can be obtained

All sorts of things can be rolled down slopes: model cars, marbles, ball-bearings, balls, tins, pieces of pipe.

How far will the truck go if it is released from   2.42
X? Does it make any difference if you put weights into the truck? Alter the slope—what effect does this have on the distance the truck goes?   2.43
(Make sure that the height of the hill is constant.)

Are there any notorious hills in your district where lorries are liable to run away?

The recording of results and events needs to be

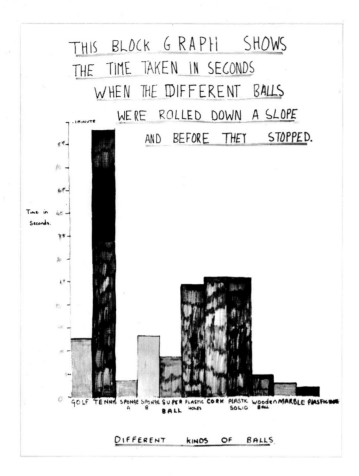

THIS BLOCK GRAPH SHOWS
THE TIME TAKEN IN SECONDS
WHEN THE DIFFERENT BALLS
WERE ROLLED DOWN A SLOPE
AND BEFORE THEY STOPPED.

Time in Seconds.

GOLF TENNIS SPONGE SPONGE SUPER PLASTIC CORK PLASTIC WOODEN MARBLE PLASTIC
A B BALL HOLES SOLID BALL

DIFFERENT KINDS OF BALLS.

Rolling balls down a slope. They were timed from the moment they started rolling until they stopped

encouraged ; not necessarily always in the same manner, but if a child has experienced something which is interesting to him he should be encouraged to communicate his findings to others, perhaps by talking about it.

1.14, 2.05, 1.73

One school devised a cardboard switchback which ran the length of the school hall. Nowdays it is easy to obtain plastic tracks and model racing cars (eg Hot Wheels, Rockets, etc) and make up switchbacks of many varieties. Here again the arrangement can be used to differing degrees of sophistication, from the measurement of time using a drip clock to, as was done in one sixth form, the measurement of time using photo transistors and an electronic counter. A switchback system using loops, hump back bridges, banked curves, a straight ending in a rising slope provides plenty of scope for an acquaintance with forces and energy.   2.44, 2.45, 3.31, 2.41, 2.58

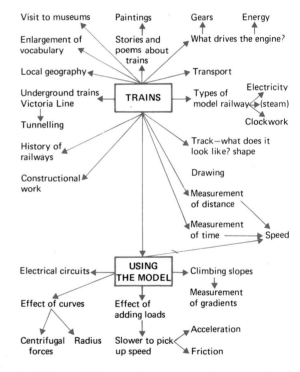

Chart of activities which have arisen from a study of toy trains

9 Toys in the playground

Out-of-door toys in a playground can provide useful experiences for children. They can explore and investigate and find out things for themselves. However, they need to be put on the right track, and the teacher needs to know what are the ideas which lie behind questions and activities.

9.1 See-saws

These are only overgrown scales. They have their classroom counterpart in the equaliser. Children can discover for themselves that two children will balance one child only when the two children are put half-way along their arm of the swing (assuming that the children are of equal weight); in other words $2 \times \frac{1}{2} = 1 \times 1$.   1.33, 1.44

Perhaps children could be asked: 2.52

Where is the hinge (pivot)? How long is the see-saw? How long are the arms? Suppose one child sat on one end, where would you sit two children *together* so that the see-saw balances? Does the see-saw swing at the same rate with two people on it, as with three?   1.71, 2.42

Could you have a see-saw with arms of unequal length?

They might compare the swinging of a see-saw with the swinging of a pendulum.   1.32

9.2 Roundabouts

We talk glibly about centrifugal force but is there such a force on a body moving round in a circle?

If a roundabout is turning, and a child hanging on at C lets go, in which direction will he be swung? If there is a centrifugal force *pulling* him outwards then he ought to move in the direction A but does he?   2.52

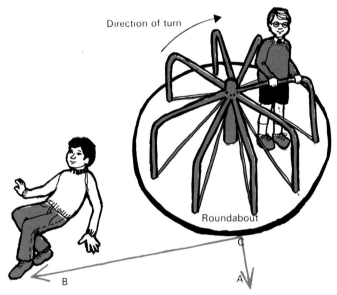

Forces work at right angles to each other on a roundabout

The roundabout keeps turning while it is being pushed but stop pushing and what happens? Why? What happens if children clamber on one side and not on the other? How is the roundabout supported?   2.52

9.3 Climbing frames

These obviously must be strong. How is this

achieved ? (See the Unit *Structures and forces Stages 1 & 2*). What are they made of ? What shape are they ? Is there a particular stable shape ? Could the children draw a diagram of one ? Could they design one they would like to play on ? Could they make a model using drinking straws ?

2.92, 1.77, 2.74

9.4 Slides

What are they made of ? Why is the slide slippery ? What polishes the surfaces ? Is it *just* the clothes ? How long does it take for a child to slide down the chute ? Does the weight of the child have any significant effect on the time of descent ?

1.59, 1.36, 2.42

9.5 Swings

These are similar in behaviour to pendulums, with two important differences :

a. The angle of swing is larger.

b. The swing is a forced one.

These factors do make the times of swings different from those of pendulums ; however, swings could provide a fruitful starting point and could be compared with pendulums in the classroom.

Is there any connection between the length of the chain, wire, rod or rope and the time of one swing ? Do heavy children swing at the same rate as light children ? Does the angle of swing have any effect on the time of swing ? 1.44, 2.41, 2.42

In pendulum and swing investigations the timing of a single swing is an inaccurate business ; this could be discussed and children might then suggest the timing of a number of swings and so find the time of one. 2.94

10 Things to make: a rag bag*

10.1 Jet-propelled car

Children have used this model for measurements of speed, distance and how much it would carry.

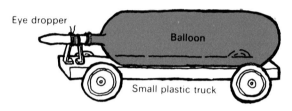

A balloon can be used to propel a small truck

10.2 Jet-propelled rocket

Two balloons can be coupled together to give a two-stage rocket. See what happens to *A* when *B* becomes deflated.

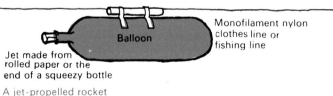

A jet-propelled rocket

A two-stage rocket

* *All these have been made by children and tested.*

10.3 Jet-propelled boat

The tubing has to be heated red-hot and then allowed to cool. This softens the metal enabling it to be bent without kinking the tubing. The ends of the tube are pushed through two holes at the rear of the boat and then soldered in place.

To make the boat go, first of all fill the spiral with water by holding one of the outlets under the tap, then put a piece of cotton wool soaked in meths under the brass spiral and light it. After a minute or so the boat will begin to move.

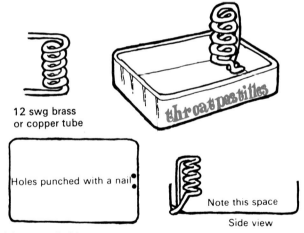

A jet-propelled boat

10.4 Fairground roundabout

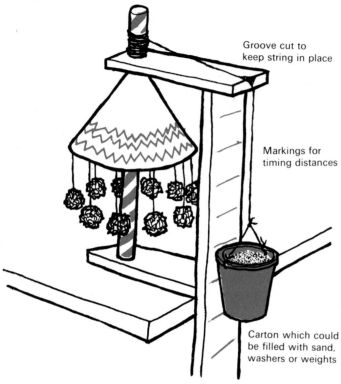

Groove cut to keep string in place

Markings for timing distances

Carton which could be filled with sand, washers or weights

Fairground roundabout operated by a falling weight

10.5 Gear-wheel systems

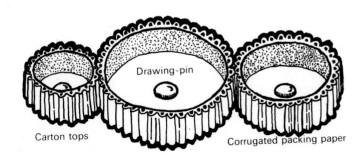

Drawing-pin

Carton tops

Corrugated packing paper

Connecting gear wheels can be made from corrugated cardboard

10.6 Dolls' house

This can be made from polystyrene ceiling tiles : the glue should be a latex glue, Evo-stik Resin W, or Lepage's 21 White Glue, or Gloy Multiglue. The type which is used for sticking polystyrene models will dissolve the expanded polystyrene. Heavy Duty Polycell can be used but it does not dry as quickly as the other two mentioned.

This project can give almost endless scope for design and improvisation. The making of furniture from match-boxes and balsa wood has proved very popular and a challenge to the children's artistic skill.

10.7 Flying models*

There is an endless variety of shapes, sizes and materials which can be used. The easiest to tackle are chuck gliders.

However, to start with, simple paper darts can be used and different shapes tried. Surprisingly enough a 50° isosceles triangle will glide if it is weighted with Plasticine or nails so that it will balance at the point X. It is rather unstable but this can be improved if a fin and rudder are added (still keeping the balancing point at X by adding more weight at the nose). Then the effects of control surfaces can be tried. Try making a glider from an expanded polystyrene ceiling tile.

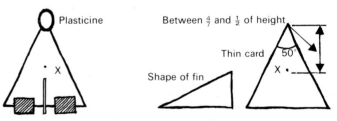

Plasticine

Between $\frac{4}{7}$ and $\frac{1}{2}$ of height

Thin card   50°

Shape of fin

Tabs of gummed tape or stiff paper

The 'chuck glider' made of a flat piece of card

Cf Solarbo Book of Balsa Models, *MAP Ltd.*

66

10.8 Plaster models

Plaster of Paris poured into a cardboard lid and then imprinted with plastic cog-wheels can produce some attractive 3D patterns, particularly if the plaster is painted with poster paints when it has set.

Another way is to put Plasticine into the lid, press the cog-wheels into the Plasticine, then use the plaster. This will produce the cast as a relief.

10.9 Hovercraft model

Mark out in pencil on a piece of stiff paper and

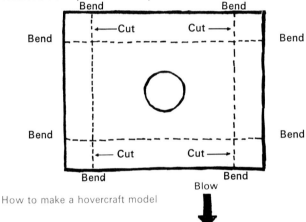

How to make a hovercraft model

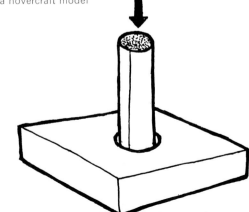

The hovercraft model can be lifted by blowing downwards

cut to size. Fold and paste the paper to form a shallow 'lid'.

Roll a piece of paper into a tube and use it to blow into the hole in the top of the lid. What happens?

Can the hovercraft be made more efficient by altering its size?

10.10 Paddle-boat, Mississippi stern wheeler

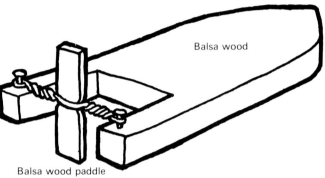

A balsa wood paddle-steamer can be powered by an elastic band

Which way does the paddle have to be wound up?

Could a four-bladed paddle be made? Does it work better? Does doubling the elastic double the speed? Does the shape of the boat have any effect on the speed?

10.11 Windmill

How can you make the propeller go faster? Is anything stopping it? (Friction.) Will a four-bladed propeller go faster? How can we make a wind in a classroom? (Either move the air or move the windmill.) Can we measure or get any idea of how much faster the windmill goes around?

In some garages a spinner something like the one above can be found. Why does it go around? It often depends on the spinner being near some obstacle so that the flow of air is uneven and there is more pressure on one half than on the other. Sometimes the spinner is deliberately bent. In this case air moving over the curve A or A' behaves in the same way as air moving over an aeroplane wing or the sails of a sailing dinghy heading into the wind, cf 6.22.

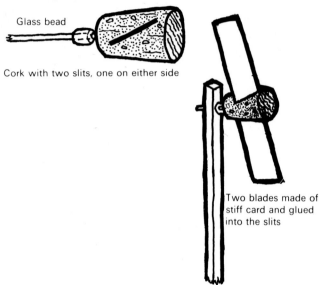

Glass bead

Cork with two slits, one on either side

Two blades made of stiff card and glued into the slits

The head of the windmill is made from cork with two card blades

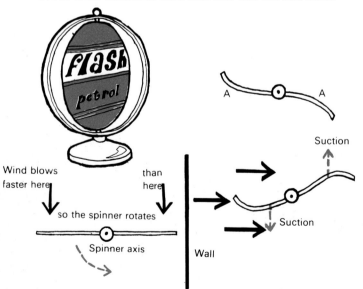

Wind blows faster here

than here

so the spinner rotates

Spinner axis

Wall

Suction

Suction

A garage spinner is rotated by uneven wind pressure

10.12 Model railway signal

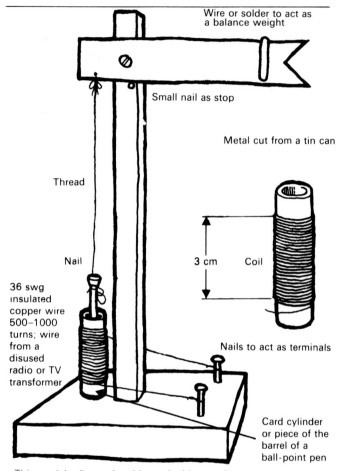

Wire or solder to act as a balance weight

Small nail as stop

Metal cut from a tin can

Thread

3 cm   Coil

Nail

Nails to act as terminals

36 swg insulated copper wire 500–1000 turns; wire from a disused radio or TV transformer

Card cylinder or piece of the barrel of a ball-point pen

This model railway signal is worked by an electro-magnet

On both the signal and the key, nails can be used as connection points to which the clips on the flex could be attached.

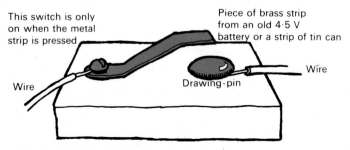

This switch is only on when the metal strip is pressed

Piece of brass strip from an old 4·5 V battery or a strip of tin can

Wire

Wire

Drawing-pin

The circuit and switch for the railway signal

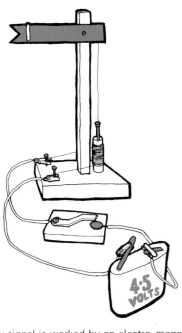

This model railway signal is worked by an electro-magnet.

10.13 The mangonel

This was an ancient siege weapon known to the Assyrians as far back as 700BC, * and was used in various forms for battering city walls and castle gates up to the time of the cannon. It was quite a formidable weapon as some versions could hurl a 25 Kg [$\frac{1}{2}$ cwt] stone 400 m [$\frac{1}{4}$ mile] and stones of about 50 kg weight have been found at High Rochester (north of Hadrian's Wall) and Camp

*See II Chronicles, xxvi. 15 and Sir Ralph W. F. Payne-Gallwey, A summary of the History, Construction and Effects in Warfare of the Projectile Throwing Engines of the Ancients, Longman, Green & Co, London, 1907.

A simple model of a mangonel which can be made very easily in the classroom

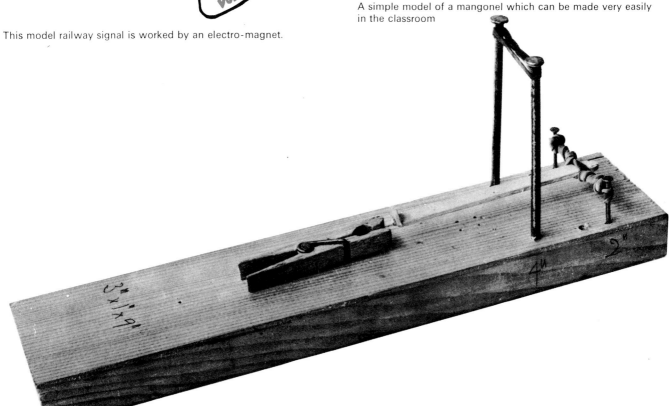

Risingham, Northumberland. It was powered by twisted hair ropes.

The first photograph shows a model which was constructed by a ten-year-old boy. The drawing is a simple version which could be made easily in the classroom. Cherry stones or dried peas make convenient ammunition.

A model mangonel made to scale by a boy of ten

FIG. 6.—SKETCH PLAN OF A CATAPULT FOR SLINGING STONES ITS ARM BEING PARTLY WOUND DOWN.

An old print of a mangonel

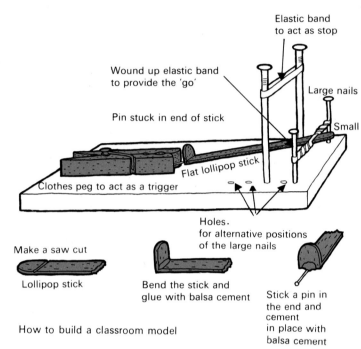

Elastic band to act as stop

Wound up elastic band to provide the 'go'

Pin stuck in end of stick

Large nails

Small

Clothes peg to act as a trigger

Flat lollipop stick

Holes. for alternative positions of the large nails

Make a saw cut

Lollipop stick

Bend the stick and glue with balsa cement

Stick a pin in the end and cement in place with balsa cement

How to build a classroom model

10.13.1 What science is there in this toy?
Observations and investigations
a. How far will a cherry stone go?
What effect does winding up the elastic have?
What effect does tilting the mangonel have?
What effect does altering the weight of the ammunition have? Try using Plasticine pellets.

b. If you keep the tension of the elastic constant, select cherry stones of the same size and keep the mangonel pointing in the same direction, do all the stones fall in the same place? Take a piece of black paper, put it on the floor and mark on it where each stone falls.

This is quite a task and requires some careful planning and deployment of labour!

What kind of pattern do you get?

c. Now pin or tape a piece of paper against the wall and find out what kind of vertical pattern is obtained. Note the mangonel will need moving towards the paper, viz the range will have to be shorter than in b : b and c could be summed up by asking what is the smallest target you could be certain of hitting, i. every time, ii. one out of every two times ?

d. Can any method be devised to find out the path of the cherry stone ? Before children try to find out ask them to draw what they think the path will be.

e. Alter the position of the large nails so that the arm of the mangonel (lollipop stick) is stopped in another position. What effect does this have on the range ?

Hidden science
a. Where does the *go* come from ?

b. Children can get experience of variables—how many different ways can you alter the range ?

(Altering the elastic tension, the weight of the ammunition, the tilt of the mangonel and the rest

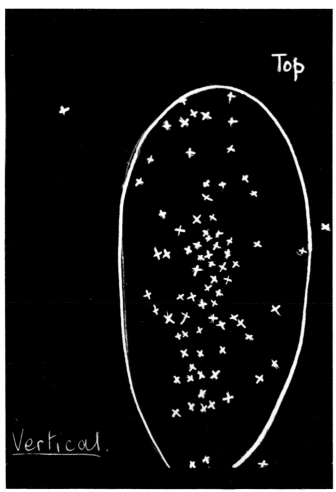

Scatter pattern of hits on a wall

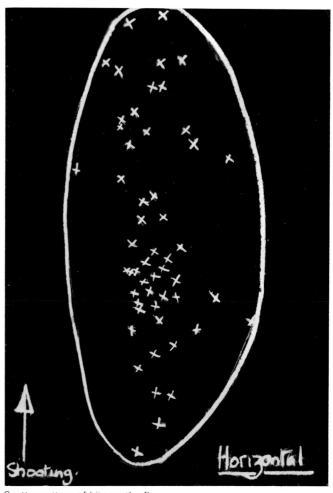

Scatter pattern of hits on the floor

position of the arm. If the arm were stopped at *B* instead of *A*, the range would be altered.)

c. The investigations provide opportunities to study the paths (trajectories) of objects thrown into the air. Many children think that things travel in straight lines not in symmetrical curves.

d. Every investigation or experiment is bedevilled with chance. Usually this is due to a combination of factors which we have either chosen to ignore because we have thought them to be insignificant, or, quite frankly, we do not know enough about them to take them into consideration. The effect of chance in this case is to make the projectiles fall within an area and not to fall at the same point. This means that an answer to the question, 'What is the range of the mangonel?' cannot be a precise one.

At the level we are working with it is inappropriate to deal with Statistics but it is appropriate to learn that in some cases there is no such thing as one 'right' answer. Also, in this case it would not mean much if we carefully measured the range of each shot, averaged them out and gave the answer to so many places of decimals. It is not much good giving the range as 4·105 m if your chance of achieving it is 1 in a 1000.

A film, *Medieval Siege Artillery,* can be hired from Educational Foundation for Visual Aids, 33 Queen Anne Street, London, W.1.

11 Appendix

11.1 List of museums

The following are museums which teachers have found to contain interesting materials—there must be many more. Is there one near you ?

Kirkstall Abbey Museum, Leeds
The Bethnal Green Museum, London
The British Museum, London
Geffrye Museum, London
Guildhall Museum, London
Museum of Childhood, Edinburgh
Museum of Costume, Bath
The London Museum
Science Museum, London
Victoria and Albert Museum, London
The Castle Museum, York

11.2 Bibliography

Books on toys fall into two categories.

a. *Books of a general nature* in which the toys are discussed from the point of view of sociology or of history.

b. *Books of a more specialised nature* in which a particular toy or type of toy is analysed, discussed and even methods of making it are shown.

11.2.1 General books
The following books are eminently suitable because not only do they give an account of toys, but they also provide a very useful bibliography.

Peepshow into Paradise. A History of Children's Toys by Leslie Gordon, published by George Halb and Co. Ltd.

A History of Toys by Antonia Fraser, published by Weidenfeld and Nicholson.

11.2.2 Specialist books
Anderson, J., *How to Make Marquetry Pictures,* M.A.P. Ltd
Anderson, R. C., *Seventeenth Century Rigging,* M.A.P. Ltd
Battson, R. K., *Period Ship Modelling,* M.A.P. Ltd
Brewer, John, *Introduction to Railway Modelling,* M.A.P. Ltd
Campbell, M. W., *Paper Toy Making,* Pitman, 1937
Chetford, Nancy, *Making Nursery Toys,* Muller, 1944
Chinn, Peter, *All about Model Aircraft,* M.A.P.Ltd.
Christopher, Catherine, *Doll Making and Collecting,* New York, 1949
Daiken, L., *Children's Toys Throughout the Ages,* London, 1953
Daiken, L., *World of Toys,* London, 1963
Deason, G. H., *Cardboard Engineering,* M.A.P. Ltd. 1958
Early, Mable, *Toy Making,* Studio, 1944
Edelman, C., *The Making of Soft Toys,* Dryad Press, 1931
Evans, Ruby, *Make Your Own Soft Toys,* Lutterworth Press, 1941
Fraser, Grace Lobbat, *Doll Making at Home,* Studio, 1940
Fritzsch, Karl E. and Bachmann, Manfred, *An Illustrated History of Toys,* Abbey Library, London
Groeber, K., *Children's Toys of Bygone Days,* London, 1932

Hallen, Julienne, *How to Make Foreign Dolls and their Costumes*, New York, 1950
Haslem, Fred, *Simple Wooden Toys*, Studio, 1945
Horton, Winifred M., *Wooden Toymaking*, Dryad Press, 1936
McCrum, J. P., *Your Toymaking*, Sylvan Press, 1951
Miall, Agnes A., *Soft Toys*, Pearson, 1950
Millward, C. N., *Modelling the Revenge*, M.A.P. Ltd
Nepean Longridge, C., *The Anatomy of Nelson's Ships*, M.A.P. Ltd
Payne-Gallwey, Sir Ralph W. F., *A summary of the History, Construction and Effects in Warfare of the Projectile throwing Engines of the Ancients*, Longman, Green & Co, Ltd, London, 1907
Pearce, Cyril, *Toys and Models*, Backsford, 1948
Polkinghorne, R. K. and M. I. R., *Toymaking in School and Home*, Hallop, revised, 1949
Priest, B. H., Mar, M. L. and Lewis, J. A., *Model Racing Yachts*, M.A.P. Ltd
Smeed, Vic, *Boat Modelling*, M.A.P. Ltd
Smeed, Vic, *Model Maker Annual*, M.A.P. Ltd
Smeed, V. E., *Power Model Boats*, M.A.P. Ltd
Turpin, Laurie, *Toys You Can Make of Wood*, Pitman, 1947
Westbury, Edgar T., *Turbines, Steam, Water and Gas*, M.A.P. Ltd
Victoria & Albert Museum, *Dolls*, H.M.S.O.
Bethnal Green Museum, *Dolls' Houses*
Victoria & Albert Museum, *Toys*, H.M.S.O.
Electric R.T.P. Flying, M.A.P. Ltd
Meccano Magazine Handbook, M.A.P. Ltd
Model Cars Encyclopaedia, M.A.P. Ltd
Model Railway Handbook, M.A.P. Ltd
Solarbo Book of Balsa Models, M.A.P. Ltd
Know your Materials: Adhesives, M.A.P. Ltd
Balsa, M.A.P. Ltd.
Hardwoods, M.A.P. Ltd.
Plastics, M.A.P. Ltd.
Metals, M.A.P. Ltd
Doping and Finishing, M.A.P. Ltd
E. Keil & Co Ltd, of Wickford, Essex, publish yearly *Keil Kraft Handbook*, which contains useful instructions and hints on modelling, together with a catalogue of tools, kits, accessories, motors, etc.

11.3 Helpful information, sources and suppliers

Paste and glues
Gloy Schools Services, Associated Adhesives Ltd, Eighth Avenue Works, Eighth Avenue, Manor Park, London, E12

Electric motors
Rip Max Ltd

Supplementary materials
1. 15 cm plastic guttering from decorator's/builder's supply merchants.
2. Model aeroplane dope/varnish; coloured oil paints; all from model shop.
3. Sheep heart—fresh from the butchers.
4. Flat elastic— $\frac{1}{8}$ in (3·5 mm), $\frac{3}{16}$ in (5 mm) from model shop.
5. Meccano parts: 22 or 23, and 18b; or (2 of 126), 21 or 22, and 18b, screws, nuts, washers.
6. Plastic pulley wheels (about $\frac{1}{2}$ in (12 mm)) obtainable from model shop.
7. 16 swg piano wire.
8. Balsa wood $\frac{1}{4}$ in $\times$ 3 in $\times$ 36 in (6 mm $\times$ 75 mm $\times$ 1 m), 1 in $\times$ 1 in $\times$ 1 in square (25 mm $\times$ 25 mm).
9. Ball-bearings of different sizes obtainable as junk from garages (do not buy new).
10. Transparent plastic sheeting such as is used for garden cloches/frames.
11. Brass curtain railing block section.
12. Planks of wood suitable for running model cars and trucks down slopes, old shelving or builders' planks.
13. 36 swg insulated copper wire—obtainable from old radio or TV sets.
14. Copper or brass tubing, internal diameter approximately 12–14 swg obtainable from model shops.
15. Expanded polystyrene, ceiling tiles and the material used for packing instruments.
16. A sheet of foam rubber.
17. Pieces of flat metal on which to drop ball-bearings, eg a piece cut from a flat spring used in a car suspension, top of an aluminium car piston, an

old flat iron, metal blocks, metal weights.
Suppliers : garages, scrap metal merchants, light
engineering works—please note only scrap
material is needed.

11.4 A note on tools for use in the classroom

1. Tenon saw for cutting hardwood.
2. Bench hook to hold wood while being cut.
3. Fretsaw, useful for cutting out shapes.
4. Balsa wood knife ; the type which uses replaceable blades is most suitable.
5. Single-edged safety razor blade.
6. Steel rule for measuring and for using as a straight edge for cutting.
7. G-clamp for holding down pieces of wood.
8. Small plane.
9. Sand-paper of various grades.
10. Stout cutting board—an old desk top.
11. Two hammers, small and medium size.

12. Two screw-drivers ; one for electrical work, ie small diameter shaft, the other for wood screws, eg no. 8, screws, 1 in [25 mm] length.
13. A Surform tool is very useful for rounding wood and for roughing out shapes.
14. A rotary drill and a set of drills suitable for metal and wood.
15. Hot wire cutter for cutting expanded polystyrene. The snags with this device are two-fold :
a. the wire easily breaks. This can be replaced by 0.20 mm iron wire supplied by BDH in 1 oz [28-g] reels. Unfortunately these are only sold in half-dozens so it might be an opportunity to ask for help from your Teacher's Centre or your nearest secondary school.
b. The cutter is intended to be run off 4.5V but it is likely to run down a dry battery fairly quickly if it is used continually for any length of time : once again the Teacher's Centre or local secondary school may be of help. See if you can borrow a 'low voltage pack', this would provide the low voltage needed by plugging into the mains.

'Lords and Commons of England, consider what nation it is whereof ye are, and whereof ye are the governors ; a nation not slow and dull, but of a quick, ingenious, and piercing spirit ; acute to invent, subtile and sinewy to discourse, not beneath the reach of any point the highest that human capacity can soar to.'
'Areopagitica', *John Milton.*

12　Index to objectives

12.1 Introduction to the index to objectives

12.1.1 Understanding the index
The index relates the *Statement of Objectives for Children Learning Science* to the Unit

It has page references to places in the Unit where ways in which children might achieve particular objectives are illustrated. The objectives are not however stated in full : for easy reference they are listed by numbers corresponding to the numbering on the main statement.

The index is not comprehensive or exhaustive.

It cannot be *comprehensive* because :

i. the objectives are but one selection of many possibilities (see page 30 *With objectives in mind*).

ii. the Units contain ideas through which many unlisted objectives could be achieved.

iii. we hope that teachers will form their own objectives.

It cannot be *exhaustive* because :

i. the written word is inadequate for conveying complete appreciation of situations which are essentially active.

ii. only the more obvious examples of activities relating to each objective are indexed : others, equally valuable, have not been cited.

The index has value only within the context of working with objects in mind
It is included to help those trying to work in this way, and suggestions for using it are set out below.

Making use of the index
The index can be used to clarify what is meant by the wording of particular objectives
The particular wording of our objectives results from trying to sum up as succinctly as possible notions which might take pages to explain fully. We think that the best way to give these statements meaning is through illustration in terms of children's activities.

In the index the entries against any one objective give page references to activities in the Unit, and each reference will show what the objective means in operation in a particular context.

By looking up several references to the same objective it is possible to build up an appreciation of what that objective means in practical terms. In this way teachers can build up operational definitions of the objectives.

The index can help understanding of the relationship which exists between objectives and activities

Objectives at the level of generality of our statements are not the kind that can be attained through a single experience. They will be achieved as a result of experience from several contributory activities. But a teacher will have many objectives

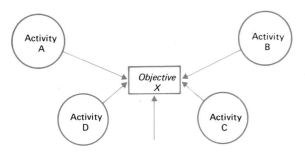

for her children in mind at any one time, and in general there is potential for working towards several objectives through any one activity :

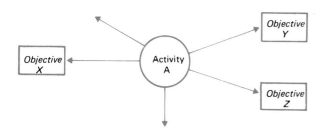

So the relationship between objectives and activities is best represented as a complex mesh :

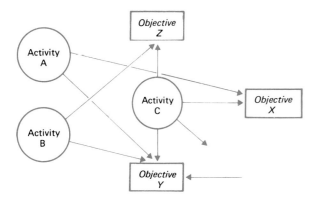

Looking through the index gives indication of this relationship : Several entries to objectives may refer to one activity. One objective has many

entries against it to different activities.

The index indicates the many different objectives to which the work of a Unit can relate

In each of the Units for teachers certain objectives are stated or referred to at several points. These are the objectives most relevant to the particular Unit, ones whose achievement is likely to be the aim of teachers when their children are working in the subject area covered by the Unit. But they are only some of the objectives which the work can help to achieve. There are many others not mentioned in the text because they are so numerous and appear so frequently that to mention them would interfere with the description of suggested activities.

Teachers will find that reference to the index brings to light the many different objectives to which the work of the Unit relates, and that it does so in a way that does not affect the continuity of the Unit.

The index can give ideas for progression towards particular objectives

When children have achieved objectives at one stage and are ready for progress towards more advanced objectives, teachers may like help with ideas of how to encourage this progression.

Suppose a child or group has reached an *awareness that more than one variable may be involved in a particular change* and the teacher feels she would like to encourage *ability to investigate variables and discover effective ones*. She may like some ideas how to guide discoveries so as to promote this. If so she may find this help by turning to examples, found by means of the Index, of activities and approaches through which the objective might be achieved in various contexts. She may or may not want to follow any of the suggestions closely, but at least she may gain ideas to apply to problems the children are currently engaged upon.

Attitudes, interests and aesthetic awareness

Objectives stated under this broad aim relate more to children's general readiness to respond in certain ways than to changes in their intellectual abilities. These objectives permeate the activities suggested in the Units to a much greater extent than do the rest of the objectives and this makes them particularly difficult to index. References to them in the text should be regarded as examples only : it is not possible for us to index any objectives comprehensively, these least of all. Indeed there are some attitude and interest objectives which are relevant to every activity ; for these it has not seemed to us appropriate to select even a few examples to note in the margins. These are such objectives :

Stage 1

1.01 Willingness to ask questions.

1.02 Willingness to handle both living and non-living materials.

1.06 Desire to find out things for oneself.

1.07 Willing participation in group work.

1.08 Willingness to comply with safety regulations in handling tools and equipment.

1.09 Appreciation of the need to learn the meaning of new words and to use them correctly.

Stage 2

2.01 Willingness to co-operate with others in science activities.

2.03 Appreciation of the reasons for safety regulations.

Stage 3

3.01 Acceptance of responsibility for their own and others' safety in experiments.

3.02 Preference for using words correctly.

We think that teachers will want to keep these objectives in mind all the time. So, to avoid constant repetition of the same numbers, references to them are not given in the margins of any text. The index, however, includes a reminder that they could be relevant everywhere.

12.2 Index to objectives of the Unit

Broad aim	Objective reference number	Page number of Unit
.30 Developing basic concepts and logical thinking (continued)	2.34 2.35 3.31 3.32	22, 25, 27, 32, 48 41, 61 62 56
.40 Posing questions and devising experiments or investigations to answer them	1.41 1.42 1.43 1.44 2.41 2.42 2.43 2.44 2.45 2.46	26, 61 25, 26, 44 22, 25, 36, 56, 60 21, 26, 44, 55, 56, 60, 63, 64 23, 41, 44, 56, 62, 64 22, 27, 43, 44, 45, 55, 56, 61, 63, 64 22, 41, 43, 46, 55, 56, 61 43, 62 62 32, 33, 41, 46
.50 .60 Acquiring knowledge and learning skills	1.52 1.53 1.55 1.56 1.58 1.59 1.63 1.64 1.65 2.51 2.52 2.53 2.55 2.56 2.58 2.59 3.52 3.56	26, 27 25 21, 26 21, 32, 36 21, 32, 45, 47, 56, 60 25, 44, 64 26 47 Everywhere 60 22, 32, 47, 48, 61, 63 22, 27, 32, 37, 47, 60 23, 37, 45 27 23, 32, 41, 45, 47, 56, 60, 61, 62 Everywhere 48, 56, 60 60
.70 Communicating	1.71 1.72 1.73 1.74 1.75	20, 48, 63 55 26, 62 21, 26, 32 21, 56

Broad aim	Objective reference number	Page number of Unit
	1.76	32
	1.77	21, 32, 64
	2.71	22
	2.72	26, 41, 44
	2.73	22, 55, 56
	2.74	22, 32, 33, 64
.80	1.81	48
Appreciating patterns and relationships	1.82	36
	2.84	23
	2.85	32, 33, 37, 48, 60
	2.86	32
	3.85	
.90	1.91	32
Interpreting findings criticially	1.92	36
	2.91	37
	2.92	41, 43, 44, 56, 64
	2.94	22, 32, 56, 64

Objectives for children learning science
Guide lines to keep in mind

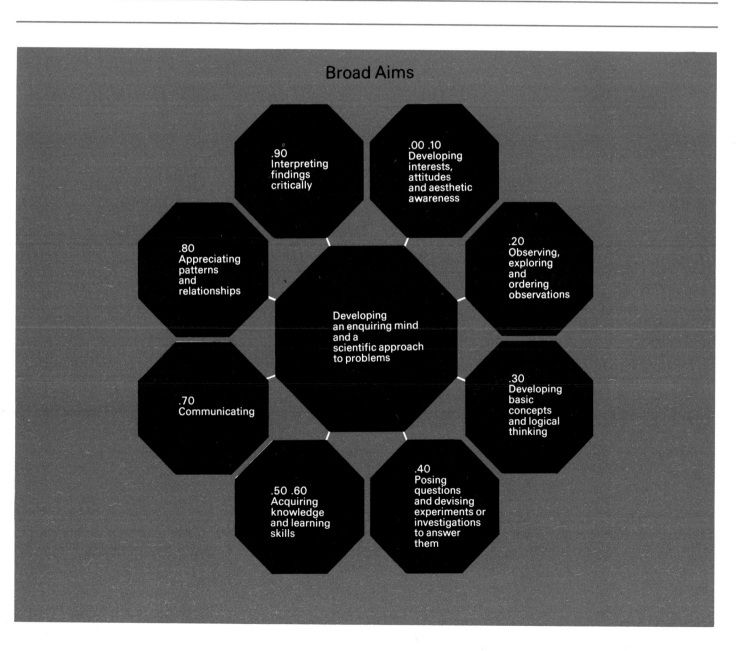

Broad Aims

.90 Interpreting findings critically

.00 .10 Developing interests, attitudes and aesthetic awareness

.80 Appreciating patterns and relationships

.20 Observing, exploring and ordering observations

Developing an enquiring mind and a scientific approach to problems

.70 Communicating

.30 Developing basic concepts and logical thinking

.50 .60 Acquiring knowledge and learning skills

.40 Posing questions and devising experiments or investigations to answer them

What we mean by Stage 1, Stage 2 and Stage 3

Attitudes, interests and aesthetic awareness

.00/.10

Stage 1
Transition from intuition to concrete operations. Infants generally.

The characteristics of thought among infant children differ in important respects from those of children over the age of about seven years. Infant thought has been described as 'intuitive' by Piaget; it is closely associated with physical action and is dominated by immediate observation. Generally, the infant is not able to think about or imagine the consequences of an action unless he has actually carried it out, nor is he yet likely to draw logical conclusions from his experiences. At this early stage the objectives are those concerned with active exploration of the immediate environment and the development of ability to discuss and communicate effectively: they relate to the kind of activities that are appropriate to these very young children, and which form an introduction to ways of exploring and of ordering observations.

1.01 Willingness to ask questions
1.02 Willingness to handle both living and non-living material.
1.03 Sensitivity to the need for giving proper care to living things.
1.04 Enjoyment in using all the senses for exploring and discriminating.
1.05 Willingness to collect material for observation or investigation.

Concrete operations. Early stage.

In this Stage, children are developing the ability to manipulate things mentally. At first this ability is limited to objects and materials that can be manipulated concretely, and even then only in a restricted way. The objectives here are concerned with developing these mental operations through exploration of concrete objects and materials—that is to say, objects and materials which, as physical things, have meaning for the child. Since older children, and even adults prefer an introduction to new ideas and problems through concrete example and physical exploration, these objectives are suitable for all children, whatever their age, who are being introduced to certain science activities for the first time.

1.06 Desire to find out things for oneself.
1.07 Willing participation in group work.
1.08 Willing compliance with safety regulations in handling tools and equipment.
1.09 Appreciation of the need to learn the meaning of new words and to use them correctly.

Stage 2
Concrete operations. Later stage.

In this Stage, a continuation of what Piaget calls the stage of concrete operations, the mental manipulations are becoming more varied and powerful. The developing ability to handle variables—for example, in dealing with multiple classification—means that problems can be solved in more ordered and quantitative ways than was previously possible. The objectives begin to be more specific to the exploration of the scientific aspects of the environment rather than to general experience, as previously. These objectives are developments of those of Stage 1 and depend on them for a foundation. They are those thought of as being appropriate for all children who have progressed from Stage 1 and not merely for nine- to eleven-year-olds.

2.01 Willingness to co-operate with others in science activitie
2.02 Willingness to observe objectively.
2.03 Appreciation of the reasons for safety regulations.
2.04 Enjoyment in examining ambiguity in the use of words.
2.05 Interest in choosing suitable means of expressing results and observations.
2.06 Willingness to assume responsibility for the proper care c living things.
2.07 Willingness to examine critically the results of their own and others' work.
2.08 Preference for putting ideas to test before accepting or rejecting them.
2.09 Appreciation that approximate methods of comparison m be more appropriate than careful measurements.

Stage 3
Transition to stage of abstract thinking.

This is the Stage in which, for some children, the ability to think about abstractions is developing. When this development is complete their thought is capable of dealing with the possible and hypothetical, and is not tied to the concrete and to the here and now. It may take place between eleven and thirteen for some able children, for some children it may happen later, and for others it may never occur. The objectives of this stage are ones which involve development of ability to use hypothetical reasoning and to separate and combine variables in a systematic way. They are appropriate to those who have achieved most of the Stage 2 objectives and who now show signs of ability to manipulate mentally ideas and propositions.

3.01 Acceptance of responsibility for their own and others' safety in experiments.
3.02 Preference for using words correctly.
3.03 Commitment to the idea of physical cause and effect.
3.04 Recognition of the need to standardise measurements.
3.05 Willingness to examine evidence critically.
3.06 Willingness to consider beforehand the usefulness of the results from a possible experiment.
3.07 Preference for choosing the most appropriate means of expressing results or observations.
3.08 Recognition of the need to acquire new skills.
3.09 Willingness to consider the role of science in everyday li

Attitudes, interests and aesthetic awareness

.00/.10

Observing, exploring and ordering observations

.20

1.21 Appreciation of the variety of living things and materials in the environment.
1.22 Awareness of changes which take place as time passes.
1.23 Recognition of common shapes—square, circle, triangle.
1.24 Recognition of regularity in patterns.
1.25 Ability to group things consistently according to chosen or given criteria.

- -

1.11 Awareness that there are various ways of testing out ideas and making observations.
1.12 Interest in comparing and classifying living or non-living things.
1.13 Enjoyment in comparing measurements with estimates.
1.14 Awareness that there are various ways of expressing results and observations.
1.15 Willingness to wait and to keep records in order to observe change in things.
1.16 Enjoyment in exploring the variety of living things in the environment.
1.17 Interest in discussing and comparing the aesthetic qualities of materials.

1.26 Awareness of the structure and form of living things.
1.27 Awareness of change of living things and non-living materials.
1.28 Recognition of the action of force
1.29 Ability to group living and non-living things by observable attributes.
1.29a Ability to distinguish regularity in events and motion.

2.11 Enjoyment in developing methods for solving problems or testing ideas.
2.12 Appreciation of the part that aesthetic qualities of materials play in determining their use.
2.13 Interest in the way discoveries were made in the past.

2.21 Awareness of internal structure in living and non-living things.
2.22 Ability to construct and use keys for identification.
2.23 Recognition of similar and congruent shapes.
2.24 Awareness of symmetry in shapes and structures.
2.25 Ability to classify living things and non-living materials in different ways.
2.26 Ability to visualise objects from different angles and the shape of cross-sections.

3.11 Appreciation of the main principles in the care of living things.
3.12 Willingness to extend methods used in science activities to other fields of experience.

3.21 Appreciation that classification criteria are arbitrary.
3.22 Ability to distinguish observations which are relevant to the solution of a problem from those which are not.
3.23 Ability to estimate the order of magnitude of physical quantities.

	Developing basic concepts and logical thinking .30	Posing questions and devising experiments or investigations to answer them .40
Stage 1 Transition from intuition to concrete operations. Infants generally.	1.31 Awareness of the meaning of words which describe various types of quantity. 1.32 Appreciation that things which are different may have features in common.	1.41 Ability to find answers to simple problems by investigatio 1.42 Ability to make comparisons in terms of one property or variable.
Concrete operations. Early stage.	1.33 Ability to predict the effect of certain changes through observation of similar changes. 1.34 Formation of the notions of the horizontal and the vertical. 1.35 Development of concepts of conservation of length and substance. 1.36 Awareness of the meaning of speed and of its relation to distance covered.	1.43 Appreciation of the need for measurement. 1.44 Awareness that more than one variable may be involved i a particular change.
Stage 2 Concrete operations. Later stage.	2.31 Appreciation of measurement as division into regular parts and repeated comparison with a unit. 2.32 Appreciation that comparisons can be made indirectly by use of an intermediary. 2.33 Development of concepts of conservation of weight, area and volume. 2.34 Appreciation of weight as a downward force. 2.35 Understanding of the speed, time, distance relation.	2.41 Ability to frame questions likely to be answered through investigations. 2.42 Ability to investigate variables and to discover effective ones. 2.43 Appreciation of the need to control variables and use controls in investigations. 2.44 Ability to choose and use either arbitrary or standard units of measurement as appropriate. 2.45 Ability to select a suitable degree of approximation and work to it. 2.46 Ability to use representational models for investigating problems or relationships.
Stage 3 Transition to stage of abstract thinking.	3.31 Familiarity with relationships involving velocity, distance, time, acceleration. 3.32 Ability to separate, exclude or combine variables in approaching problems. 3.33 Ability to formulate hypotheses not dependent upon direct observation. 3.34 Ability to extend reasoning beyond the actual to the possible. 3.35 Ability to distinguish a logically sound proof from others less sound.	3.41 Attempting to identify the essential steps in approaching a problem scientifically. 3.42 Ability to design experiments with effective controls for testing hypotheses. 3.43 Ability to visualise a hypothetical situation as a useful simplification of actual observations. 3.44 Ability to construct scale models for investigation and to appreciate implications of changing the scale.

Acquiring knowledge and learning skills

.50/.60

1.51   Ability to discriminate between different materials.
1.52   Awareness of the characteristics of living things.
1.53   Awareness of properties which materials can have.
1.54   Ability to use displayed reference material for identifying living and non-living things.

- -

1.55   Familiarity with sources of sound.
1.56   Awareness of sources of heat, light and electricity.
1.57   Knowledge that change can be produced in common substances.
1.58   Appreciation that ability to move or cause movement requires energy.
1.59   Knowledge of differences in properties between and within common groups of materials.

1.61   Appreciation of man's use of other living things and their products.
1.62   Awareness that man's way of life has changed through the ages.
1.63   Skill in manipulating tools and materials.
1.64   Development of techniques for handling living things correctly.
1.65   Ability to use books for supplementing ideas or information.

2.51   Knowledge of conditions which promote changes in living things and non-living materials.
2.52   Familiarity with a wide range of forces and of ways in which they can be changed.
2.53   Knowledge of sources and simple properties of common forms of energy.
2.54   Knowledge of the origins of common materials.
2.55   Awareness of some discoveries and inventions by famous scientists.
2.56   Knowledge of ways to investigate and measure properties of living things and non-living materials.
2.57   Awareness of changes in the design of measuring instruments and tools during man's history.
2.58   Skill in devising and constructing simple apparatus.
2.59   Ability to select relevant information from books or other reference material.

3.51   Knowledge that chemical change results from interaction.
3.52   Knowledge that energy can be stored and converted in various ways.
3.53   Awareness of the universal nature of gravity.
3.54   Knowledge of the main constituents and variations in the composition of soil and of the earth.
3.55   Knowledge that properties of matter can be explained by reference to its particulate nature.
3.56   Knowledge of certain properties of heat, light, sound, electrical, mechanical and chemical energy.
3.57   Knowledge of a wide range of living organisms.
3.58   Development of the concept of an internal environment.
3.59   Knowledge of the nature and variations in basic life processes.

3.61   Appreciation of levels of organisation in living things.
3.62   Appreciation of the significance of the work and ideas of some famous scientists.
3.63   Ability to apply relevant knowledge without help of contextual cues.
3.64   Ability to use scientific equipment and instruments for extending the range of human senses.

Communicating

.70

Appreciating patterns and relationships

.80

Stage 1 Transition from intuition to concrete operations. Infants generally.	*1.71* Ability to use new words appropriately. *1.72* Ability to record events in their sequences. *1.73* Ability to discuss and record impressions of living and non-living things in the environment. *1.74* Ability to use representational symbols for recording information on charts or block graphs.	*1.81* Awareness of cause-effect relationships.

- -

Concrete operations. Early stage.	*1.75* Ability to tabulate information and use tables. *1.76* Familiarity with names of living things and non-living materials. *1.77* Ability to record impressions by making models, painting or drawing.	*1.82* Development of a concept of environment. *1.83* Formation of a broad idea of variation in living things. *1.84* Awareness of seasonal changes in living things. *1.85* Awareness of differences in physical conditions between different parts of the Earth.

Stage 2 Concrete operations. Later stage.	*2.71* Ability to use non-representational symbols in plans, charts, etc. *2.72* Ability to interpret observations in terms of trends and rates of change. *2.73* Ability to use histograms and other simple graphical forms for communicating data. *2.74* Ability to construct models as a means of recording observations.	*2.81* Awareness of sequences of change in natural phenomena *2.82* Awareness of structure-function relationship in parts of living things. *2.83* Appreciation of interdependence among living things. *2.84* Awareness of the impact of man's activities on other living things. *2.85* Awareness of the changes in the physical environment brought about by man's activity. *2.86* Appreciation of the relationships of parts and wholes.

Stage 3 Transition to stage of abstract thinking.	*3.71* Ability to select the graphical form most appropriate to the information being recorded. *3.72* Ability to use three-dimensional models or graphs for recording results. *3.73* Ability to deduce information from graphs : from gradient, area, intercept. *3.74* Ability to use analogies to explain scientific ideas and theories.	*3.81* Recognition that the ratio of volume to surface area is significant. *3.82* Appreciation of the scale of the universe. *3.83* Understanding of the nature and significance of changes in living and non-living things. *3.84* Recognition that energy has many forms and is conserved when it is changed from one form to another. *3.85* Recognition of man's impact on living things—conservation, change, control. *3.86* Appreciation of the social implications of man's changing use of materials, historical and contemporary. *3.87* Appreciation of the social implications of research in science. *3.88* Appreciation of the role of science in the changing pattern of provision for human needs.

Interpreting findings critically

.90

1.91   Awareness that the apparent size, shape and relationships of things depend on the position of the observer.

1.92   Appreciation that properties of materials influence their use.

2.91   Appreciation of adaptation to environment.
2.92   Appreciation of how the form and structure of materials relate to their function and properties.
2.93   Awareness that many factors need to be considered when choosing a material for a particular use.
2.94   Recognition of the role of chance in making measurements and experiments.

3.91   Ability to draw from observations conclusions that are unbiased by preconception.
3.92   Willingness to accept factual evidence despite perceptual contradictions.
3.93   Awareness that the degree of accuracy of measurements has to be taken into account when results are interpreted.
3.94   Awareness that unstated assumptions can affect conclusions drawn from argument or experimental results.
3.95   Appreciation of the need to integrate findings into a simplifying generalisation.
3.96   Willingness to check that conclusions are consistent with further evidence.

These Stages we have chosen conform to modern ideas about children's learning. They conveniently describe for us the mental development of children between the ages of five and thirteen years, but it must be remembered that ALTHOUGH CHILDREN GO THROUGH THESE STAGES IN THE SAME ORDER THEY DO NOT GO THROUGH THEM AT THE SAME RATES.
SOME children achieve the later Stages at an early age.
SOME loiter in the early Stages for quite a time.
SOME never have the mental ability to develop to the later Stages.
ALL appear to be ragged in their movement from one Stage to another.
Our Stages, then, are not tied to chronological age, so in any one class of children there will be, almost certainly, some children at differing Stages of mental development.

Illustration acknowledgements:

The publishers gratefully acknowledge the help given by the following in supplying photographs on the pages indicated:

The trustees of the British Museum, 2, 3, 70

Chatham Standard, 1

Corgi Toys, 18

South West Picture Agency, 11, 12, 14, 26, 28, 32, 35, 42, 44, 52, 53, 58, 62, 69, 70, 71

Scala, Milan, opposite page 4

The Victoria and Albert Museum, 70

Line drawings by The Garden Studio: Helen Jackson

Cover design by Peter Gauld

Index